WITHDRAWN

POWER FOR THE PEOPLE

POWER FOR THE PEOPLE

Trevor Cairns

Published in cooperation with Cambridge University Press

Lerner Publications Company, Minneapolis

LIBRARY OF CONGRESS CATALOGING IN PUBLICATION DATA

Cairns, Trevor.
    Power for the people.

    (The Cambridge Introduction to History, v. 8)
    Includes index.
    SUMMARY: Discusses the industrial development, political
movements, and rise of nationalism in 19th-century Europe.

    1.   Europe—History—1789-1900—Juvenile   literature.
2.   France—History—Revolution,   1789-1799—Influence—
Juvenile literature. [1. Europe—History—1789-1900] I. Title.

D358.5.C33 1980   940.2'8   79-2973
ISBN 0-8225-0808-7

This edition first published 1980 by Lerner Publications Company
by permission of Cambridge University Press.

Copyright © MCMLXXVIII by Cambridge University Press.
Original edition published as part of *The Cambridge Introduction to the History of Mankind.*

International Standard Book Number: 0-8225-0808-7
Library of Congress Catalog Card Number: 79-2973

Manufactured in the United States of America.

This edition is available exclusively from:
Lerner Publications Company, 241 First Avenue North, Minneapolis, Minnesota 55401

1 2 3 4 5 6 7 8 9 10 85 84 83 82 81 80

Contents

Below: *If any one day can be recognised as the beginning of the railway age, it must be 27 September 1825, when the Stockton and Darlington Railway was formally opened. This contemporary print shows part of the train, which consisted of twelve wagons for goods and twenty-two for passengers.*

List of Maps and Diagrams

Editors' Note: In preparing this edition of *The Cambridge Introduction to History* for publication, the editors have made only a few minor changes in the original material. In some isolated cases, British spelling and usage were altered in order to avoid possible confusion for our readers. Whenever necessary, information was added to clarify references to people, places, and events in British history. An index and a list of maps and diagrams were also provided in each volume.

All references to money in this book are given in British monetary units. The basic unit is the pound (£), which is equal to 20 shillings (s) or 100 pence (d). In recent years, the value of the British pound has varied from about $2.50 to about $1.50 in U.S. currency.

Acknowledgments

Illustrations in this volume are reproduced by kind permission of the following:
Front cover, pp. 13 (Telford's aqueduct), 45 (Chartist riots) National Museum of Wales, Cardiff; p. 1 Borough of Darlington Museum; pp. 3, 8 (loom), 10, 11, 40 Crown Copyright. Science Museum, London; p. 4 (Constable) Ipswich Museums; p. 4 (Indian) India Office Library & Records; p. 4 (African) Peter Fraenkel's Photographs; p. 5 (post mill) Jeffrey W. Whitelaw; p. 5 (watermill) Emrys Jones; pp. 7, 8 (lady spinning, jenny), 15, 26, 31 (Makriyannis), 41 (workhouse interior and exterior), 45 (meeting), 46, 47, 49 (Dickens), 51, 53 (boy), 70 (lily bracket), 71 (cartoon, Greek slave), 74, 78 (bow-wow), 91 Cambridge University Library; p. 8 (flying shuttle) Calderdale Museums Service; p. 9 Waterways Museum, Stoke Bruerne; pp. 12 (mail coach), 13 (charges document) 92 (penny black) The Post Office; p. 12 (Arkwright's mill) Derby Museums and Art Gallery; p. 17 (Coke of Holkham) Viscount Coke (photo Campbell MacCallum); pp. 17 (Farmer George), 20, 37 The Trustees of the British Museum; p. 19 from the Institute of Bankers' Collection of Paper Money; p. 21 Royal Pavilion, Art Gallery and Museums, Brighton; pp. 24 (Beethoven), 27 (Metternich), 32 (Louis Philippe), 34, 42, 48, 59 (Francis Joseph), 83, 90 Mansell Collection; p. 24 (waltzers) Mosco Carner, *The Waltz* (Max Parrish, 1948); p. 25 (Lorelei) Glasgow Art Gallery; p. 25 (Turner) reproduced by courtesy of the Trustees, The National Gallery, London; pp. 27 (Byron), 92 (Queen Victoria), 95 The National Portrait Gallery, London; pp. 31 (Charles X), 41 (monitorial system), 50, 58 (Radetzky), 65 (Pope), 66, 82, 86, 88 (barricades) Radio Times Hulton Picture Library; p. 32 (Liberty) Clichés Musées Nationaux Paris; p. 43 Trades Union Congress; p. 49 (The Eviction) University College, Dublin (photo Green Studio); pp. 52 (photo Holzapfel), 54 (October entry and eagles) Documentation Française; pp. 53 (fighting, Bibliothèque Nationale), 79 (Boulevard, Musée Carnavalet) Photographie Lauros-Giraudon; p. 54 (Louis Napolcon) Bibliothèque Nationale, Paris; pp. 57 & 65 (costume, photo John Freeman), 69, 70 (agricultural machinery, envelope machine, fireplace), 71 (traffic) Crown Copyright. Victoria and Albert Museum; p. 58 (Kossuth) Österreichische National-bibliothek; p. 59 (execution) National Széchényi Library, Budapest; p. 60 Ullstein Bilderdienst; p. 62 British Library; p. 67 *Historia y Vida*, Barcelona; p. 68 (Victoria) reproduced by gracious permission of Her Majesty the Queen; p. 68 (Marx) Marx Memorial Library, London;
p. 72 Sheffield City Libraries; p. 73 (Keble College) William Shepherd; p. 73 (Methodist Chapel) Conrad Cairns; p. 76 National Maritime Museum, London; p. 77 photo John Beecham; p. 78 (Dunant) British Red Cross Society; p. 79 (Etoile) Aerofilms Limited; p. 80 Collection Bertarelli, Milan; p. 87 Fried Krupp GmbH, West Germany; p. 88 (La Revanche) Musée des Arts Decoratifs, Paris; p. 89 Museen der Stadt Wien; p. 92 (European postage stamps) Stewart Arrandale; p. 96 Ironbridge Gorge Museum Trust.

Maps and diagrams by Reg Piggott and Leslie Marshall

front cover: *Sometimes during the long French wars the British government could not mint enough small coins to meet the needs of commerce and industry, and local firms met this shortage by issuing their own tokens, which could be redeemed for ordinary money. This one was issued in 1813. It illustrates the growing power of industry: the workmen are rolling out wrought iron between cast-iron rollers which are worked by a large toothed wheel, itself probably driven by a watermill.*

back cover: *The triumph of nationalism, celebrated on the cover of part of a children's pictorial history of the Fatherland, published during the Second Reich. The coming together of the Germans as a united people is symbolised by the handshake of a Bavarian and a Prussian. It was a union, as the title puts it, 'bought with the blood of heroes' in the war of 1870–1.*

1 A new way for people to live: Britain 1750–1820

above: *An English village: East Bergholt, Suffolk, painted about 1812 by John Constable, 1776–1837. It is part of the view from a window in his father's house.*

below: *An Indian village: Ghour, Uttar Pradesh, painted about 1825 by Captain James Manson.*

Life as it always had been

These villages may look different, but they stand for the same thing. People must eat. The food must come from the land. Thinkers and writers, artists and builders, statesmen and soldiers, those who have made and marred cities and states and civilisations – they all have relied upon villagers tilling the land and tending the animals. Craftsmen and merchants in their teeming markets, from Peking to Timbuktu to London, prospered only because the peasants were able to produce enough extra rice or corn or meat to feed them.

Thus it had been since men in the New Stone Age had first farmed and dwelt in towns. There remained wide tracts of the world's surface where the people remained hunters, food-gatherers, nomadic herdsmen, but wherever people led a settled life most of them were countryfolk. In the eighteenth

below: *An African village: photograph of traditionally built Hausa dwellings near Saria, Nigeria.*

century perhaps eight out of every ten Europeans lived in villages, hamlets or isolated farmsteads.

They depended on nature. If the crops failed there would be want, hardship. If they failed for two or three successive years there would be famine, death. It was simply a fact of life. So was the death-rate among young children; most babies failed to grow up. Apart from killers like the plague and smallpox, people suffered from lesser ailments with few remedies. An obviously decayed tooth might be dragged out, some village women might be skilled in brewing herbs to alleviate fevers or heal wounds; physicians and surgeons were expensive, and often enough seem to have done little other than increase the patient's sufferings. People accepted it. They had to. It would have been as useful to complain about such things as to complain about being alive.

Townsmen and nobles and kings may have enjoyed more comfort and luxury, but the realities of disease and death were the same for them, too.

On the other hand nature gave gifts for people to use. They built their houses from the natural materials they found locally. They used the natural strength of animals, of water and wind.

People knew how to multiply such natural strength by means of levers and pulleys, but only one artificial form of power had been invented by humans and successfully put to work: gunpowder.

It would be a simple though lengthy task to list the differences between that way of life and life in present-day highly developed industrialised societies. We need not assume that the new is better or happier than the old; that is a matter for argument. There can be no question, however, about the gigantic size and quantity of changes. The events which brought about this new way of life for a great part of humanity—perhaps for the entire human race, eventually—are called the Industrial Revolution. It is easy to see why it has sometimes been described as the most important thing in history, after the so-called Neolithic Revolution, when people learned how to farm.

It started in late Stuart and Hanoverian Britain, without anybody realising what was happening.

left: *Rossett Watermill, Clwyd (1661). This is an undershot mill, so called because the water strikes the wheel from below.*

far left: *Pitstone Green Windmill, Ivinghoe, Bucks., built probably in 1627. This is a post mill, so called because the whole body is mounted on a huge post (here it passes through the white base) and can be swivelled so that the sails catch the wind well.*

5

below left: *Savery Engine. The vessel was first filled with steam and then cooled by water. This cooling condensed the steam, causing a vacuum which sucked the flood-water into the vessel through the suction pipe. When more steam was let into the vessel, it pushed the water up the forcing pipe and out. The diagram is greatly simplified. In the real engine there were two boilers and vessels acting alternately.*

below right: *Newcomen Engine. The beam operated a pump which was at the bottom end of the rod; it was weighted so as to rest with this arm down. The cylinder was filled with steam. When the steam was condensed (in this case by water sprayed inside) there was a vacuum, so the pressure of the air outside thrust down the big piston, thus moving the beam and so operating the pump. This type of engine is technically not a steam engine but an atmospheric engine, because the piston is moved not by steam but by the pressure of the atmosphere.*

Revolutions in work

Machines show their power

PUMPING WITH STEAM ENGINES. In Cornwall they had mined tin since the Bronze Age, going deeper and deeper until at last water, seeping into the workings, threatened to make further mining impossible. Pumping by muscle-power, as sailors pumped ships, was too weak for such depths. Pumping is a straight up-and-down movement. What the mine-owners needed was something that could give a mighty push, withdraw, push, withdraw, push . . .

The late seventeenth century was a time when many of the foremost men in Europe were interested in scientific ideas and experiments. Perhaps it was this background of thought that encouraged Thomas Savery, a military engineer who had already invented a method of paddling boats, to apply steam power to the problem. Hero of Alexandria had experimented

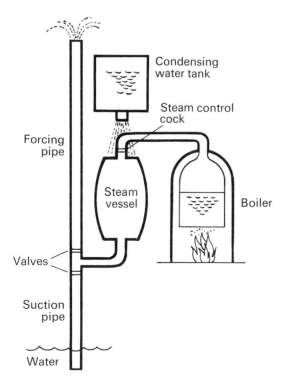

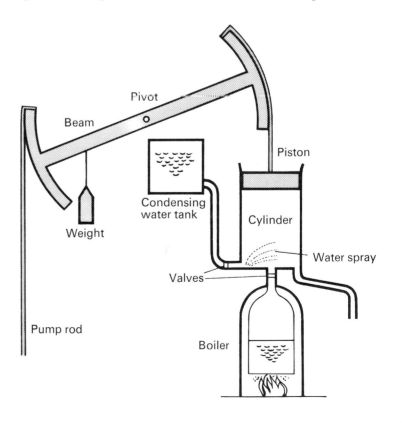

successfully with steam 1,800 years before, and his writings were known to Renaissance scholars, but nobody had yet been able to do anything useful with steam. In 1698 Savery succeeded. His machine was clumsy and slow. At every suck the steam in the vessel had to be cooled back into water and then the refilling began, which was very wasteful and slow. But the mines needed strength, not speed.

Within seven years Thomas Newcomen produced a new engine which, though still clumsy and slow, proved strong and serviceable. Humans now had a power far greater than their own or animals' muscles (Savery had no way of measuring the strength of his machine, so he reckoned it in 'horse-power') and which could, unlike winds and streams, be applied and controlled when and where it was needed. This power was super-human, in one sense super-natural. Though at present it was limited to straight up-and-down motion, from now on people would certainly strive to master this tremendous power and make it serve them in many other ways.

SMELTING WITH COAL. Iron had been the supreme metal ever since human beings had learned to smelt it, cheap, tough and, when necessary, deadly. However, its quality varied widely, depending not only on the quality of the original ore and skill of the smith, but also on the smelting. Impurities in fuel, for example, might pass into the metal and render it brittle. Therefore iron-founders used pure charcoal, and preferred to work in heavily wooded country. But by about 1700 wood was being used alarmingly faster than new trees could grow. The wood shortage affected all sorts of people. Shipbuilders wanted British oak for their hulls, while depending on imports from the Baltic for most of their masts and yards. Householders in London burned coal in their hearths, not wood: sea-coal, it was called, because it came from Newcastle in sturdy little boats. Laws to prevent Londoners from poisoning the air with the stinking sooty stuff had all failed because there simply was not enough wood fuel.

Those impurities which polluted London made coal unsuitable for use in smelting iron. Then, early in the eighteenth century, a Shropshire iron-founder named Abraham Darby came up with the idea of treating coal as wood was treated to turn it into charcoal, that is, burning it with the minimum of air. The result was coke, and it proved pure enough to be used in smelting. Darby's works at Coalbrookdale prospered.

Soon another method of using coal was developed, the blast furnace. Here the idea was to pump air through the fire until it became so hot that impurities were forced out, falling into the slag or shooting up the chimney.

There was no shortage of ore or coal, so cast iron could be produced more readily than ever before. In making steel or wrought iron there was still no substitute for the skilled craftsman's hands, but the basic material for hundreds of everyday articles was more plentiful and thus cheaper.

above: *Charcoal-burning, shown here from the great French Encyclopaedia of the mid-eighteenth century, was a job requiring skill and patience. If all went well, a large cone of wood was reduced to a small mound of charcoal.*

below: *Diagram, also from the Encyclopaedia, of a blast furnace. It shows in section the huge toothed wheel, itself driven by a waterwheel, which raised and lowered the levers operating the bellows. Though only one of these can be seen in the diagram, there were two bellows operated alternately so that a steady blast of air could be maintained.*

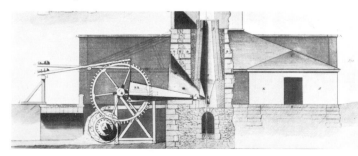

MACHINES FOR MAKING CLOTH. When one of George I's subjects bought a coat he paid for a little wool and a lot of labour. The wool had grown on small, skinny sheep. It had been sheared by hand, cleaned and sorted by hand, carried on pack-horses' backs to cottages where women and children spun it, one thread at a time. Then it went to the weaver, sitting at his loom, passing the shuttle, which carried the weft thread from side to side, in and out between the warp threads. And so the different processes went on, carding and fulling and dyeing, until the finished roll of woollen cloth reached the tailor.

For several centuries wool had been England's main trade. First it had been exported raw, to the clothmakers of Flanders in the Middle Ages. Then a clothmaking industry had grown prosperous in England itself, mainly in the Cotswolds, East Anglia and Yorkshire. During the seventeenth century cotton cloth had increasingly been made in Lancashire; it was relatively cheap and washable, but the cotton thread often proved too weak to be used as warp, so that wool or linen threads had to be substituted and mixed cloth, such as fustian, was produced.

Spinning the thread and weaving it into cloth were the two most important processes. Both were laborious, but one weaver could use up all the thread from a number of spinners. In 1733 William Kay invented a device which allowed the weaver to work faster. This was his 'flying shuttle' which was flicked across the loom mechanically instead of merely by hand.

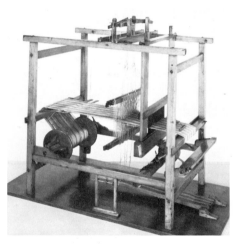

Weaving *Sitting at the near end of his hand-loom the weaver threw from side to side the shuttle carrying the weft thread, between the rows of warp thread. The 'flying shuttle' (below, enlarged) was driven across the guide-beam with the aid of spring-operated levers on each side.*

Spinning *These two pictures from E. Baines' 'History of the Cotton Manufacture in Great Britain', 1835, show how the spinning wheel 'only admitted of one thread being spun at a time by one pair of hands', while the jenny (below), likewise operated by one wheel, was a device 'by which twenty, fifty, a hundred or even a thousand threads could be spun at once by a single pair of hands'.*

In 1738 there was an attempt to improve spinning. Lewis Paul and John Wyatt patented the idea of twisting the strands over rollers and thus making the thread stronger. The idea was sound, though the early machines were too clumsy to succeed. The next step was taken by a weaver and carpenter named James Hargreaves, who in the early 1760s made a spinning 'ingenium' or 'jenny'. A legend grew up that he got the idea when his wife's spinning wheel was knocked over and he saw it from a new angle, but he had already been employed by a clothmaker named Robert Peel to improve other machines. The jenny allowed a spinner to make several threads at once.

Some people feared – and with reason – that inventions which allowed one man or woman to produce more would automatically mean that other men and women would find themselves with no work. Both Kay and Hargreaves had their machines wrecked by mobs. But it is not so easy to destroy ideas. By the late 1780s there were said to be 20,000 jennies in use.

CHEAP BULK TRANSPORT. For moving big, heavy cargoes water was the easiest, cheapest method, and this had been appreciated for centuries. Coal was such a cargo. By the middle of the eighteenth century the demand for it was growing. The Duke of Bridgewater owned mines at Worsley, near Manchester, and wanted to move his coal along the River Mersey. However, one company had been given, by Parliament, a monopoly of the river traffic in return for keeping the river clear and safe, and the company charged the Duke a heavy fee. So the Duke consulted an engineer, James Brindley, who in 1759 designed for him his own waterway – a canal.

In world history, from Egypt and China to the Netherlands and France, canals were an old idea, but this was the first serious attempt to build one in Britain since Roman times. It was necessary to get Parliament's permission because a canal, like a road, would interfere with the legal rights of the people through whose land it passed. The Duke had a struggle, because the Mersey Navigation Company objected furiously, but he won and built his canal. Once built, a canal can be reasonably cheap to run. Bridgewater not only carried his coal cheaply, but ran passenger barges cheaply and still made a good profit. As trade in bulky objects increased, companies were launched to follow the Duke's example.

These were the key inventions. They showed that

steam power was a practical possibility,

iron could be plentiful (coal already was),

machines could multiply the production of cloth,

transport of heavy loads could be cheap.

As people put together these ideas and others like them, and worked them out, a revolution gradually took place in British industry.

The basin of the Grand Junction Canal at Paddington, 1801. If this print is to be believed, the buildings, boats and activity provided an agreeable sight for strolling Londoners.

'Daily inventing . . .'

In 1752 a book on trade and manufactures referred to 'infinite numbers daily inventing new machines'. Literary exaggeration, no doubt, but it did reflect a fashionable attitude. Many practical and ingenious people were coming to believe in the opportunities for improvement. They saw the chance to create things of their own, out of their own brains, and to enrich themselves at the same time. So new ideas sprouted in many industries and trades. A brief account of what happened to the 'big four' should indicate how things were being transformed.

Steam engines and their manufacture were so improved in so many ways by James Watt (1736–1819) that people sometimes think of him as the true inventor of steam power. Watt realised the need for converting the straight thrusts of the engine into a circular movement that would drive the wheels of other machines, but, as a French inventor had already patented the crank action, Watt had to produce a rather more elaborate alternative. This ability to overcome problems enabled him to make his engines much more economical and reliable than the earlier types – and he, in his turn, patented his ideas so that they could be used only by people who were prepared to pay him. Other inventors wanted engines to turn wheels on which the engines themselves were mounted, and so create *loco motives* capable of pulling heavy loads. Again a French inventor was first, but although his artillery tractor worked there were too many problems about employing it on active service. In France, also, there was a successful steamboat, but this too did not seem worth the trouble and expense of developing. This was France of the old regime, soon to be convulsed by revolution. In Britain there were men who, despite repeated failures, continued to push their experiments towards efficient steam locomotion.

Iron manufacture continued to improve. Henry Cort (1740–1800) was probably the most important innovator with his process of puddling (stirring) the molten metal and rolling it as it cooled, thus mixing and pressing it into greater strength. New foundries sprang up in many places as new uses were found for this most useful of materials.

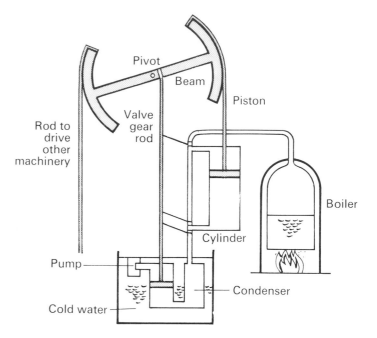

right: *Model of 'Old Bess', a Watt engine built in 1777, which was used until 1848 for pumping water at a factory near Birmingham. The pipe bringing steam from the boiler is on the right, the water-wheel which turned the machinery on the left.*

left: *Watt Engine. This retains many features of the Newcomen engine, but one great difference is that by a system of valves the steam is made to push the piston down and, in the more advanced models, both up and down. This, therefore, is a true steam engine. The used steam is led into a separate condenser to be cooled into water, and can then be pumped back into the boiler for re-use. Besides being connected to the piston and to the driving gear for other machinery, the beam operates rods controlling the valves (shown) and the pumps (not shown).*

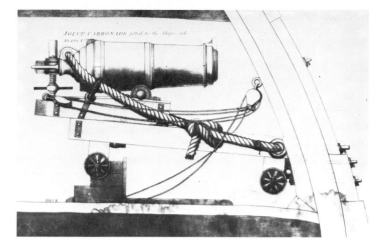

Two early attempts to design steam locomotives. William Murdock, an assistant of Watt, made the model on the left in 1786; it worked, but he did not develop it, and his main achievement was the invention of coal-gas lighting. On the right is a model of a differently designed engine by Richard Trevithick, a Cornish mining engineer, about 1800. Trevithick pioneered the use of high-pressure steam, made many models, and built some of the earliest practical locomotives.

The Carron Ironworks, near Falkirk, produced a new type of gun which was cheap, light, short, easy to handle and capable of firing much heavier shot than ordinary guns of comparable size. Though there was a disadvantage — the range was relatively short — it became widely used at sea in the late eighteenth century. It was called a carronade.

Carronade sizes and weight of shot

Weight of shot	Diameter of bore	Length of carronade There were even shorter versions.
68 pounds	8.05 inches	62 inches
42	6.84	51.5
32	6.35	48.5
24	5.68	43.5
18	5.16	39
12	4.52	26

right: *The Coalbrookdale Ironworks, in Shropshire, spanned the Severn Gorge in 1773–9 with the first cast-iron bridge in the world. The parts were designed and fitted together according to the time-honoured principles of wooden construction, but eventually engineers realised that iron, having different qualities from wood, could be used in different designs. The bridge still stands in excellent condition.*

Cloth remained Britain's principal manufacture and therefore attracted many would-be inventors. One of the most successful was Richard Arkwright, once a barber, who in 1769 produced a machine which made twisted thread by means of rollers – the idea which Paul and Wyatt had tried with less success. By 1771 this machine had been adapted so that it could be driven by water, as in a water-mill; it was now called a water-frame. It marked a turning point. Machines like this could not be fitted into a spinner's home. People who worked them had to go where the machines were, in the mill.

The third great spinning invention was Samuel Crompton's, in 1779. Both the jenny and the frame had defects. The first produced brittle thread, the second coarse. Crompton tried to combine the good qualities of both machines, and since the result was cross-bred he called it a mule. It made thread that was both fine and strong.

Weaving was different. The skill of a weaver's hands was too complex to be imitated by a machine, so people believed. Then the Rev. Edmund Cartwright took up this challenge to his ingenuity, and by 1789 he had won. He invented a power loom. At first the power was intended to be provided by an animal, but soon the loom was adapted for water-power, and steam.

Arkwright's cotton mill at Cromford, Derbyshire, as shown in a water-colour by William Day about 1789. Since the streams in hilly country provided the best power, it was not unusual for mills to be sited in places which could appear picturesque or even romantic.

Transport seemed an excellent investment as trade increased. People with money to invest eagerly bought shares in canal companies, to such an extent that the 1790s saw what has been called the 'canal boom'. In fact they over-invested, so that many canal companies could not earn a profit and went bankrupt. But by the end of the century the main manufacturing areas of Britain were well supplied with waterways, either natural or artificial.

Good roads were still needed. For many years Parliament had been willing to allow groups of men to build good stretches of road and repay themselves by charging tolls. The revolving spikes over the toll-gates were known as turnpikes, and the name became applied to the roads themselves, while the groups responsible for them were called turnpike trusts. The trusts sometimes employed outstanding engineers, like Thomas Telford (1787–1834) and John Loudon Macadam (1756–1836). Telford's work was careful, solid and often beautifully proportioned, like that of the ancient Romans. Macadam, in contrast, experimented until he found a way of making a smooth, strong, durable surface cheaply. He packed granite chippings tightly together so that the traffic would press them more firmly still. The fine new surfaces encouraged coach-builders to design lighter, faster and very elegant vehicles; the early nineteenth century was to be the great age of British coaching.

DOVER

MAIL.	Miles	Pence
Ashford	58	8
Canterbury	56	8
Chatham	31	7
Dartford	15	5
Deal	74	8
Dover	72	8
Feversham	47	7
Folkestone	79	8
Gravesend	22	6
Hithe	68	9
Maidstone	38	7
Margate	79	8
New Romney	92	9
Queenborough	49	7
Ramsgate	75	8
Rochester	29	6
Sandwich	68	8
Sheerness	51	8
Sittingbourne	40	7
Wingham	62	8

POOL

MAIL.	Miles	Pence
Alresford	60	8
Alton	50	6
Bagshot	29	6
Bishops Waltham	78	8
Bracknell	31	7
Christchurch	110	9
Farnham	41	7
Isle of Wight	95	9

EXETER *continued.*

	Miles	Pence
Kingsbridge	220	11
Launceston	216	11
Lyme	146	10
Marazion	289	12
Newton Abbot	192	11
Oakhampton	198	11
Odiam	43	7
Overton	56	8
Penryn	260	12
Penzance	292	12
Salisbury	84	9
St. Columb	252	12
Shaftesbury	104	9
Sherborn	119	9
Sidmouth	188	11
Stockbridge	79	8
Teignmouth	192	11
Truro	260	12
Topsham	180	11
Totness	203	11
Weymouth	181	10
Whitchurch	60	8
Yeovil	125	10

TAUNTON

COACH.	Miles	Pence
Bradford	105	9
Bridgewater	150	10
Collumpton	182	11
Devizes	92	9
Froome	115	9

SHREWSBURY *continued.*

	Miles	Pence
Beaconsfield	26	6
Bicester	70	8
Bishop's Castle	166	10
Bridgenorth	148	10
Cirencester	94	9
Dursley	114	9
Ellesmere	181	11
Fairford	85	9
Farringdon	75	8
Gerrard's Cross	23	6
Highworth	81	9
High Wycomb	32	6
Kenton	89	9
Lechlade	81	9
Minchinhampton	104	9
Newport	155	10
Oswestry	182	11
Oxford	57	8
Shiffnall	146	10
Shrewsbury	165	10
Stokenchurch	39	7
Southall	12	4
Stratford on Avon	99	9
Stroud	109	9
Thame	40	7
Tetbury	104	9
Tetsworth	45	7
Uxbridge	18	5
Wantage	73	8
Welchpool	183	11
Wellington	146	10
Wheatley	51	8

LIVERPOOL *continued.*

	Miles	Pence
Warwick	107	9
Watford	18	5
Wendover	40	7
Winslow	53	8

CHESTER

MAIL.	Miles	Pence
Atherstone	108	9
Ampthill	49	7
Bangor	248	12
Beaumaris	255	12
Burton	194	10
Carnarvon	257	12
Chester	190	11
Conway	252	12
Drayton	155	10
Denbigh	224	11
Dunatable	34	7
Hinckley	100	9
Holywell	208	11
Holyhead	275	12
Leighton Buzzard	49	7
Luton	39	7
Lutterworth	89	9
Namptwich	169	10
Newport Pagnel	51	8
Ruthin	231	12
St Asaph	218	11
Stafford	141	10
Tamworth	116	9

above: Part of a table of mileages and postal charges between 1812 and 1839. There is a separate heading for each coach service out of London.

left: On a moonlit night the mail coach from Edinburgh comes to the Stamford Hill Turnpike, near London, and the gatekeeper emerges from his cottage to open the gate. A coloured engraving by G. Hunt, published about 1829.

below: One of the masterpieces of Thomas Telford, the Pontcysyllte Aqueduct near Acrefair, carrying the Shropshire Union Canal across the valley of the Dee. A coloured engraving by F. Jukes after J. Parry, 1808.

Transport in Britain, about 1830

——	Canals	
——	Navigable rivers	
——	Post roads	

0 — 100 miles
0 — 150 km

It is very likely that by 1800 Britain was already making, carrying and trading more intensively than any country before. Yet the Industrial Revolution had hardly begun to hint at the effects it would have in the following century.

Farming for profit

When we talk about Industry we often exclude the biggest and most basic industry of all: farming. Perhaps this is because we think of industry as making the things we use, and of farming as growing the things we eat. Perhaps it is because, partly as a result of the Industrial Revolution, we are in the habit of thinking of industry as something that goes on in big towns.

As long as towns had existed they had contained people who did not produce their own food, but relied on nearby farmers bringing their surplus crops and animals to sell or exchange in the market. The bigger towns grew, the more they demanded. By 1600 there were about 150,000 Londoners who needed food even more than fuel (see page 7), and farmers in most of the south-eastern English counties sent in their produce, often by barge. Sussex sent wheat especially, Essex oats, Suffolk butter. In 1615 a market was begun at Smithfield entirely for the animals which had been herded, often from distant counties, to supply the capital with meat. Though London was by far the largest, other towns likewise had many mouths to feed.

Landowners large and small, from lords to yeomen, became increasingly interested in *improving* – a word that was to be fashionable for a long time. In other countries, and most obviously just across the sea in the Netherlands, farmers had been forced for generations to make the best use of their limited land by draining, by experimenting with new crops in new rotations, by planting in orderly rows. However, what suited one type of soil and weather need not suit another, and small farmers could not always afford the expenses and risks involved. Therefore the example was set by large landowners who wished to increase the value of their property.

Most prominent among the early eighteenth-century improvers was Charles, Viscount Townshend, nicknamed 'Turnip'. A great Whig lord and member of Walpole's government, he quarrelled with the Prime Minister and resigned in 1730. Then he devoted his energy and intelligence to his estates in Norfolk. Turnips were one of the new crops which improving farmers had been trying in experimental rotations since the previous century. The idea was to find some way of using the land every year, instead of leaving much of it to rest fallow as in the medieval system which was still widely followed. If different crops drew different substances from the soil, then by care-

fully arranging the order in which they followed one another in a field, and by good manuring, farmers could use all their arable land instead of only two thirds each year. A four-year rotation became popular, and it was known as the Norfolk Four Course System.

Not all ideas spread rapidly. In 1731 another intelligent and successful landowner, Jethro Tull of Wiltshire, published *Horse-Hoeing Husbandry*. It described how to use horse-drawn machines in spacing rows of plants and weeding between the rows. Some of Tull's ideas were admired, but it was a century before his seed-drill came into general use.

Many of the new root crops, like rutabagas and beets, were valuable for feeding animals. This feed not only made them fatter, but also made it easier to keep them alive through the winter. As late as the end of the century there were areas where one third of the cows and horses had to be slaughtered each autumn for lack of winter feed, but generally by then there had been great improvements in stock-farming, and new strains of animals were bred. The best-known breeder was Robert Bakewell, who farmed at Dishley, Leicestershire. He succeeded with sheep, cows and horses; by 1789 he could charge a fee of 1,200 guineas for the use of three rams for one season's breeding. The revolution in animal breeding meant a great improvement in the supplies of meat and of dairy products.

The new farming was not for poor people, because the farmer needed to begin with money and fields. Imagine a peasant trying to introduce new methods on his strips on the open field, or breed better animals on the village common. Of course there were parts of the country where open fields had never been usual, and other parts where open fields had been enclosed into private fields in the fifteenth and sixteenth centuries. Then it had been mainly for sheep-rearing (for wool, not mutton), and only partly to feed growing towns. Now the demand was mainly for food, and landowners wanting to profit from new methods thought it necessary to get rid of the many open fields which remained. They wanted the land to be redistributed so that every land holder received one united area instead of scattered strips, and would keep this permanently. In any particular parish if everybody who had a share agreed, so much the better. But otherwise the would-be enclosers could still get their own way, for Parliament had the power to pass an act enclosing the land. Between the beginning

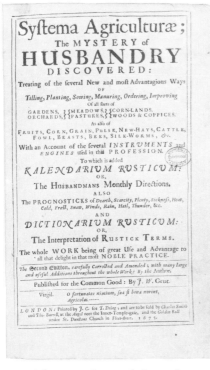

Syſtema Agriculturæ;
The MYSTERY of
HUSBANDRY
DISCOVERED:

Treating of the ſeveral New and moſt Advantagious Ways
OF
Tilling, Planting, Sowing, Manuring, Ordering, Improving
Of all ſorts of
GARDENS, ⎱ ⎰ MEADOWS, ⎱ ⎰ CORN-LANDS,
ORCHARDS, ⎰ ⎱ PASTURES, ⎰ ⎱ WOODS & COPPICES.

As alſo of
FRUITS, CORN, GRAIN, PULSE, NEW-HAYS, CATTLE,
FOWL, BEASTS, BEES, SILK-WORMS, &c.

With an Account of the ſeveral INSTRUMENTS and
ENGINES uſed in this PROFESSION.
To which is added
KALENDARIUM RUSTICUM:
OR,
The Husbandmans Monthly Directions.

ALSO
The PROGNOSTICKS of Dearth, Scarcity, Plenty, Sickneſs, Heat,
Cold, Froſt, Snow, Winds, Rain, Hail, Thunder, &c.

AND
DICTIONARIUM RUSTICUM:
OR,
The Interpretation of Rustick Terms.

The whole WORK being of great Uſe and Advantage to
all that delight in that moſt NOBLE PRACTICE.

The Second Edition, carefully Corrected and Amended; with many large
and uſeful Additions throughout the whole Work: By the Author.

Publiſhed for the Common Good: By J. W. Gent.

Virgil. O fortunatos nimium, ſua ſi bona norint,
Agricolas.——

LONDON: Printed by J. C. for T. Dring; and are to be ſold by Charles Smith
and Tho. Burrell, at the Angel neer the Inner-Temple-gate, and the Golden Ball
under St. Dunstans Church in Fleet-ſtreet. 1675.

The title page of one of the early 'improving' books, first published in 1669 and reprinted several times. The author was John Worlidge of Petersfield, Hampshire.

TEES-WATER OLD OR UNIMPROVED
BREED.

THE largest breed of Sheep in this island is to be met with on the banks of the Tees, which runs through a rich and fertile country, dividing the two counties of Yorkshire and Durham. This kind differs from the Lincolnshire Sheep, in their wool not being so long and heavy; their legs are longer, but finer boned, and support a thicker, firmer carcase; their flesh is likewise much fatter, and finer grained.

Our figure was taken in July, 1798, from a Ram which had been purchased for the purpose of shewing its uncouth and uncultivated appearance, in contrast to those of the improved kind.

TEES-WATER IMPROVED BREED.

By persevering in the same laudable plan of improvement so successfully begun by the late Mr Bakewell, the stock-farmers or graziers of Tees-water have produced a kind which is looked upon by judges as nearly approaching to perfection. Many of their Sheep possess the thriving or fattening quality of the Dishley breed, and are fit for the butcher at as early an age.

These Sheep weigh from twenty-five to forty-five pounds per quarter; some have been fed to fifty pounds; and one in particular was killed, which weighed sixty-two pounds ten ounces per quarter, avoirdupois; a circumstance never before heard of in this island. The Ewes of this breed generally bring forth two lambs each season; sometimes three, four, and even five. As

A pair of pages from Thomas Bewick's 'History of Quadrupeds', 1807 edition, published in Newcastle upon Tyne.

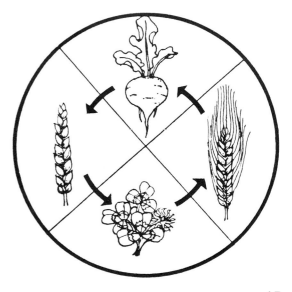

The main idea of the Norfolk Four Course Rotation (right) was to alternate cereals like wheat and barley with root crops and clovers. As a result it was no longer necessary to leave a field lying fallow every second or third year.

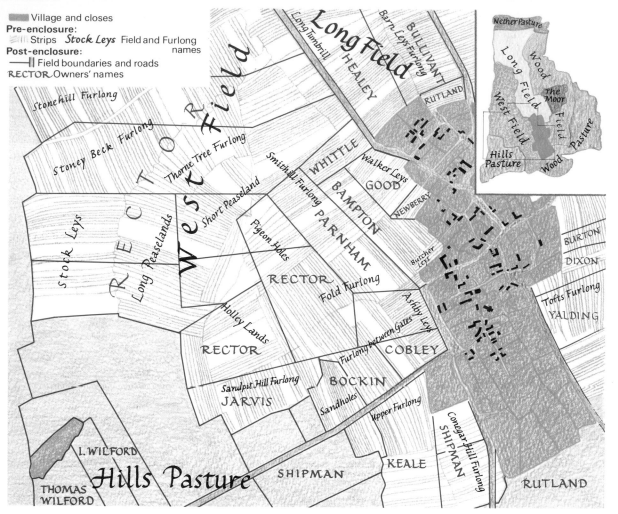

Stathern, Leicestershire, was enclosed in 1792 and these maps are redrawn from surveys made then. The smaller map shows the pre-enclosure village and its fields as a whole. The other is an enlargement of a part, showing how the redistribution of the land worked out. The scale of the large map is about 7 inches to 1 mile (11 centimetres to 1 kilometre).

of the eighteenth century and the end of the Napoleonic Wars about $2\frac{1}{2}$ million acres (over 1 million hectares) were enclosed by agreement and $5\frac{1}{2}$ million acres ($2\frac{1}{4}$ million hectares) by Act of Parliament. It was this which created what people today sometimes regard as the typical English landscape, a comfortable sight with its neat patchwork of fields and hedgerows and substantial farmhouses. The picture may be misleading in some ways, for local conditions caused wide variations, and often there was little cosiness for the countryman. On the whole it seems likely that those who received only small farms in the enclosure awards could not succeed, and that the winners were the larger landowners and their tenant farmers.

Agriculture was booming, and the government recognised its national importance. The agricultural writer Arthur Young edited forty-seven volumes of *Annals of Agriculture* between 1784 and 1809. He became secretary of the newly founded Board of Agriculture in 1793 and organised a survey of British agriculture, one volume per county. Meanwhile in the 1790s the president of the Board, Sir John Sinclair, was producing

right: *'Coke of Holkham at the Sheep Shearing',* a painting by T. Weaver, made in 1808.

below: *The king himself was seriously interested in agricultural improvement and gave a lot of attention to his farm at Windsor. Sometimes he was nicknamed 'Farmer George'. This cartoon of 1786 shows George III and Queen Charlotte as a farmer and his wife.*

another agricultural survey in his *Statistical Account of Scotland.* Scottish farmers took up the new methods so enthusiastically that for many years they were the most efficient in Britain, and Scots were employed to manage farms in other parts.

Farming was fashionable, too. Country dress was worn in London, even in Paris. So much did it become the English style that the symbol of Britain, John Bull, still wears it. At the turn of the century, British agriculture seemed to be personified in the figure of 'Coke of Norfolk'. Thomas Coke (1752-1842) was an influential member of Parliament (M.P.) and the wealthy owner of palatial Holkham Hall, and he earned fame as the most enthusiastic and magnificent of all improving landlords. Every year he held a great assembly in the lordly halls of Holkham. Guests, many of them highly distinguished, came from all parts of Britain and, indeed, Europe to this festival, the Holkham sheep-shearing. The principle topic of conversation was agriculture.

Going to Market.

Why did it happen?

By the end of the eighteenth century the increase in trade and industry was very obvious, even if nobody could foresee how gigantic the effects would become. Why had this revolution begun in Georgian Britain?

Inventions and experiments arise from ideas in human minds. It may not be possible to explain why one person gets an idea and follows it through, while another fails to see the idea or, if he sees it, fails to develop it. However, throughout history there have been people trying to make things easier or better, and succeeding; with writing in ancient times, for example, or architecture in the Middle Ages. Since the time of Leonardo da Vinci and Copernicus many highly intelligent men had been applying their minds to what we would now probably call scientific subjects, and often working in a scientific manner – searching, questioning, imagining, testing.

During the seventeenth century many important scientific

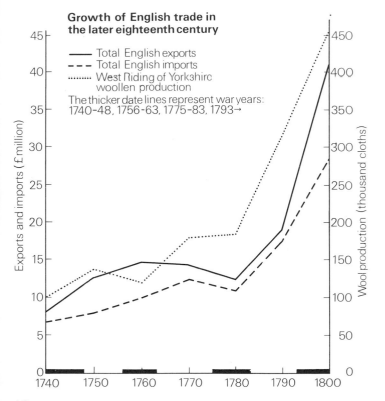

Growth of English trade in the later eighteenth century

— Total English exports
--- Total English imports
.... West Riding of Yorkshire woollen production

The thicker date lines represent war years: 1740-48, 1756-63, 1775-83, 1793→

Exports and imports (£ million)

Wool production (thousand cloths)

discoveries were made by men of many nations. The Englishman Harvey discovered how the blood circulated (1616) and the Dutchman Leuwenhoek with his microscope accurately described the red corpuscles (1674). The Scotsman Napier worked out tables of logarithms (1614) and the German Leibnitz introduced the differential calculus (1684). Most famous of all, the Italian Galileo (1564–1642) experimented with lenses, pendulums and falling objects, and had a long struggle with the Church because some of his ideas about the universe seemed not to agree with Scripture. In the later part of the century British scientists were encouraged by the Royal Society (founded 1662) and the most famous of them was Isaac Newton (1642–1727). He did not merely lay down the law of gravity, but a complete theory of physics which scientists generally accepted until well into the twentieth century.

Scientific advances led to agricultural and industrial advances, but indirectly. Though, for example, the Royal Society in 1664 began a survey of agricultural methods in order to seek improvements, on the whole scientists did not devise new practical processes. It can be argued, however, that they created the right 'intellectual climate' without which the practical inventors would not have flourished.

Ideas and plans would remain ideas and plans unless people had the means to turn them into reality. In the late seventeenth century and early eighteenth, many people in Europe seem to have been eager to throw their money into very optimistic schemes for making fat profits. Partly the reason may have been that the Spanish monopoly in the New World was apparently cracking, and there were wildly exaggerated estimates of vast wealth easily tapped. In 1695 thousands of Scots put their savings into the Darien Scheme, for a colony strategically placed to control the vital Isthmus of Panama. Fever and the Spaniards destroyed the settlement and the investors lost everything they had staked. Meanwhile the Bank of England, also founded in 1695, was laying solid foundations as a national financial centre which could issue banknotes and lend support to business enterprises. Ironically both the incomparably successful bank and the totally disastrous scheme came from the brain of the same man, William Paterson. Another Scotsman, John Law, founded the General Bank in France in 1716, and began his Mississippi Scheme the following year. The scheme was wildly popular and ill-judged; it collapsed in 1720, ruining thousands. In England, that was the year when

The Bank of England had no monopoly of issuing notes, and local banks were very important in financing businesses. This 1838 note was issued by one such bank, which was eventually absorbed into the National Provincial, later the National Westminster Bank.

the 'South Sea Bubble' burst, with similar effects. This occurred because Spain had agreed to permit a very limited amount of trade in South American waters, and investors fell into a sort of craze, believing that the opportunities were enormous. Naturally, there were dishonest financiers to encourage this folly, and the crash when it came was cruel. Though many paid the penalty for judging wrongly, it seems clear that there was a great deal of money about, in the hands of people looking for profitable investments. In other words, capital was available.

An industry needs people at both ends: at one end to produce and sell, at the other to buy and consume. Much could be sold overseas, in Asia or America, and money earned there could become capital for more industry, but the main market was at home. At this time populations were increasing, in country and town alike, at a rate never known before. It is estimated that the population of England and Wales in 1500 was about $4\frac{1}{2}$ millions and by 1700 had only increased to about $5\frac{1}{2}$ millions. In 1801, when the first census was taken, it was 8,896,723. The need for food, clothes, shelter – and jobs – was growing faster than ever before.

Why was the population increasing with such impetuous speed? There is no certain answer as to why people breed more

less, but there have been several theories about this period. ne is that better supplies of food helped many more children survive; thus it could be said that the Agricultural Revolution produced its own customers. It has also been argued that workers in new industrial conditions reached the peak of their earning power when they were young, and therefore tended to marry earlier and produce larger families. Was the Industrial Revolution also producing its own customers? One thing that seems unquestionable is that medicine was becoming better though the main effects of this were probably not felt until the nineteenth century. The most obvious example is smallpox, which had been the great killer disease; inoculation against it began in the 1720s, and in 1798 Dr Edward Jenner published his discovery of vaccination. It is possible that the death-rate was falling and the birth-rate rising at the same time, and that in some places one cause was more significant than in others.

These conditions, though, were not peculiar to Britain, so why did the Industrial and Agricultural Revolutions occur there? France especially could be thought more likely – bigger, richer, the cultural centre of all Europe. The great French Encyclopaedia contained an unequalled range of technical information and diagrams; Frenchmen led the way in steam transport and ballooning. But French society was probably not really interested; the aristocracy at the top and the peasantry at the base provided neither leadership nor support. In Britain, unlike other countries, only the eldest son of a lord became himself a peer; the rest of the family often found it wiser, therefore, to forget the prejudices of nobility and join the money-makers. The gulf between aristocrats and the rest could also be bridged from the other side, by those with enough talent and luck. Sir Robert Walpole was a country gentleman, the Pitts had made their money in the East India trade, Lord Chancellor Eldon was the son of a coal-merchant, and Arkwright the barber ended as Sir Richard, High Sheriff of Derbyshire.

Where such complicated and far-reaching changes are concerned, it is only to be expected that the causes should appear many and involved: availability of raw materials and money; improvements in farming, manufacture, transport; more people to buy and to work; leaders willing to take advantage of changes. Other countries had many of these, but it happened to be Britain where they all clicked together and began the Agricultural–Industrial Revolution.

The pressure of war

The graphs on page 18 partly show when Britain was at war during the eighteenth century. This was a time that has sometimes been called the Second Hundred Years' War against France. By 1763 Britain had won what is often known as the First British Empire, and twenty years later the War of American Independence had broken it. At this time colonial empires were still being governed by their mother countries according to the mercantilist theory: strict customs barriers intended to protect trade and industry within the empire and to keep foreigners from sharing this wealth. You may think it possible to judge from the graphs whether or not wars and empire had much effect on British trade. Remember, though, that these are only a few sets of statistics, and that there could be all sorts of factors sending the figures up or down, or cancelling one another out.

Whatever the figures may mean, there is no doubt that in the later part of the century a new idea about trade was gaining strength. In *The Wealth of Nations*, published in 1776, a professor of Glasgow University named Adam Smith argued that trade caused an increase in the wealth of everybody concerned – the more trade, the more wealth for each. So it was a mistake for a country to try to wall in its industries against competition. Instead it should throw open its trade so that its people could buy the cheapest and best, wherever it came from; and so that its manufacturers and merchants would have to work well in order to match foreign competition, while they would have the opportunity of selling freely in wide foreign markets. Smith's book had tremendous influence. One result was that political economy, or economics as it is now termed, came to be accepted as a separate subject to be studied at universities. More practically, William Pitt the Younger, Prime Minister from 1783, proclaimed himself a disciple of Adam Smith, and began to reduce tariff barriers.

It was a time when change and improvement seem to have been in the air at Westminster. Parliament was constantly passing bills for improvements like turnpikes and enclosures, as we have seen, while there were philanthropist M.P.s pressing for the abolition of the slave trade and slavery in British colonies. Some M.P.s, including Pitt, thought that Parliament should improve itself; it should deprive little and corrupt boroughs of their M.P.s, and give the seats to counties.

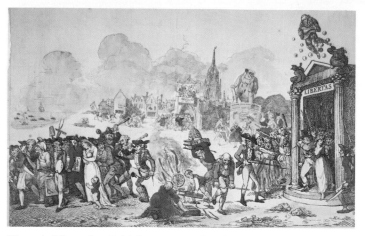

'French Liberty', a British cartoon of 1793. Some revolutionaries are driving Liberty from her temple and preparing to kill her, while others are burning books and instruments of science, art and industry; decent people of all sorts are being forced to go away. The idiotic harlequin above the temple is the notorious English revolutionary writer, Tom Paine.

Then the French Revolution broke out.

At first France seemed to be ruled by moderates, constitutional reformers who wanted a parliamentary monarchy like Britain's. Naturally many British of all classes, including the rulers, approved of such very sensible conduct. But when extremists seized power and blood flowed, especially royal and aristocratic blood; and when they recklessly challenged the might of other European monarchies, and won; then the attitude of Britain's rulers changed to horror and alarm. 'Jacobinism' was, after 1793, seen as a menace to decent civilised life – as lived by the ruling classes. In 1797 the menace seemed to become more dire when a mutiny paralysed the fleets at Spithead and the Nore. However, most of the ordinary people of Britain seem to have shared their rulers' loathing of the French. They saw the revolutionaries not as liberating comrades but as pillaging oppressors trying to conquer the free British people. Even the naval mutineers assured their officers, whom they treated with respect, that if the French fleet dared to put to sea they would sail at once to sink it. Nevertheless, the following year a rebellion blazed out in Ireland, encouraged by the French, and was only quelled after serious fighting.

The great war against Revolutionary and then Napoleonic France lasted from 1793 to 1814, with only one interval from March 1802 to May 1803. The Industrial Revolution had not changed the methods of warfare. Nelson's ships and guns were much the same as Hawke's or Rodney's, and the 'Brown Bess' musket of Wellington's men had already been 'the infantryman's best friend' for a century. (Napoleon, too, cared little for new devices; for example, he rejected a steamship and a submarine proposed by an American called Robert Fulton.) In less obvious ways, though, the changes which had taken place in British agriculture and industry may have been what saved her now. Food was often scarce, but the farmers were able to produce more than ever before—especially because they hoped to get a high price for it. Armies, both British and foreign, needed uniforms, equipment, weapons; the textile and metal industries throve. Some historians think that the wars earlier in the eighteenth century may have slowed the industrial changes, by causing rich men to lend money to the government instead of investing it in business. But this war seemed to be having a very different effect, for there was money for both. The government was able to raise unheard-of sums of money, partly by taxation (income tax was introduced in 1798), partly by borrowing (the national debt more than tripled between 1792 and 1815). Some of the money was needed to persuade allies to begin or continue fighting.

For the lucky ones, it was a good war. The Prince Regent (his father, George III, was still king, but subject to fits of apparent madness) set the pace. He was at the centre of an extravagant, often dissolute, but elegant and fashionable society. Regency comfort and elegance, though not its wildness, spread through the middle classes. There were dangers, of course. A merchant could make a fortune, but just as easily lose everything if his cargoes were snapped up by the fast French privateers that infested the Channel. Competition was keen. There were many bankruptcies. But these were merely the casualties, easily forgotten. In the middle-class drawing rooms which Jane Austen meticulously described in her novels, war and work seemed not to exist.

Among the poor it was very different. In Berkshire some farm workers were not being paid enough to keep them alive, and their employers said that they simply could not afford higher wages. So the local magistrates in 1795, meeting at Speenhamland, near Newbury, decided to supplement low

The Prince Regent discovered a quiet rustic retreat in a farmhouse at the fishing village of Brighton. He converted it into a fantastic pseudo-oriental 'pavilion', shown here in a coloured engraving from a book published by the main architect, John Nash, in 1826. Nash also designed Regent's Park and Regent Street in London.

wages from local property taxes, so that each worker should have just enough to feed his family. The Speenhamland system spread to other counties. In the towns, too, there was hardship, and here the workers were much more crowded together than in the countryside. In 1799 and 1800 the government, nervous about treasonable plots, introduced the Combination Acts, which forbade people to combine in any form of conspiracy, whatever its purpose. As a result, it was now illegal for workmen to form a union to bargain for better wages from their employers. Discontent boiled over in 1811 in textile and similar manufacturing areas. Food was expensive. New machines were putting some men out of work and forcing other to accept lower pay. Beginning in Nottinghamshire but soon spreading to Lancashire, Cheshire and the West Riding of Yorkshire, organized crowds smashed and burned machines. They called themselves Luddites, after a mythical leader, 'King Lud' or 'General Lud'; some said they were named after an idiot lad called Ned Lud who had wrecked a machine in a fit of rage. Troops soon put down the riots, and machine-wrecking was added to the long list of crimes for which free Britons could be hanged while Britain was fighting for freedom against France.

Post-war discontent

After two decades of war the change to peace in 1815 upset a lot of things that people had become used to. Obviously the armed forces shrank rapidly, and thousands of men had to find new jobs as civilians. Similarly the forces no longer were ordering the boots and coats, ships and wagons, guns and sabres that they had urgently bought for twenty years. Manufacturers had to seek new markets, possibly in Europe, where it was once more safe and legal to trade. Farmers and landowners also had their worries. They had cultivated extra land, some of it of low quality, because of the wartime demand for food, and they had been able to make this pay because they could rely on steady good prices. Now corn (grain) could be shipped in from Europe, and British farmers no longer enjoyed a virtual monopoly; could they afford to reduce their prices to match the lower expected prices of foreign corn?

The government was very sympathetic over the plight of the landed classes. The Houses of Lords and Commons were full of landowners whose incomes would decline if their tenant farmers could no longer manage to pay high rents. But there was another reason for trying to protect British agriculture. In time of war it was dangerous to have to rely on imported food, as everyone had learned. During the recent war there had been bad shortages, and the population went on increasing while the usable land did not. It would be reckless not to look after the food supply. Already there had been a warning in 1813, when a sudden fall in prices after a good harvest had ruined many farmers and country bankers. Therefore, in 1815 Corn Laws were passed to keep the prices up. Foreign corn would not be allowed into Britain until prices rose to 80 shillings per quarter—very near famine price. Prudent statesmanship it may have been, but to poor people who could hardly afford their daily bread, it seemed callous.

In fact, during those years the price of corn never rose to anywhere near that limit. Generally prices, which had nearly doubled during the war, fell back almost to what they had been in 1793. With the employers suffering such losses, the workers they employed were sure to suffer too. Meanwhile the population continued to soar. There were more and more consumers, people who needed food and clothing and shelter—and jobs. But they did not have the money to buy what they wanted, and while trade was depressed there was no more work to be found.

Discontent might become dangerous. The poor were being pushed, massed into towns. According to the 1811 census over a million people lived in London and its suburbs; Edinburgh and Glasgow, Manchester and Liverpool had all passed 100,000, while Birmingham was 85,000 and rising fast (it was over 100,000 by 1821). Besides, numbers of smaller manufacturing towns were grouped quite close together around centres like Birmingham or Manchester, or in regions like the West Riding, while coalfields were sprouting pit villages. In such regions it was easy for news and rumours and complaints to spread, and for plotters to find fellow-conspirators, for orators to find audiences, for leaders to find followers. Discontented crowds could be stirred up, could feel the strength of their numbers, could feel anonymous and safe, could turn into rioting, destructive mobs. In the growing industrial districts the ordinary people were being gathered into masses, and this gave them the possibility of a power they had never possessed before. They also had reason to want to use power.

There was great cause for discontent. Besides unemployment and low wages, people often endured disgusting living places. People were increasing so fast that housing, hurriedly and cheaply built, was almost bound to be nasty – a problem that was to persist for many generations. Many were huddled into decaying old houses in town centres or into hastily built cheap, new, dingy streets and suburbs that soon became just as squalid. People often had to work all the day and half the night, and bring their children to work too, if they wanted to eat.

Poverty in the countryside was at least as bad. It was from the wretchedness of the countryside that many of the poor of the towns had come to seek work, for there was no hope in their native villages. In town and country alike life looked very grim for a large number of poor people; perhaps – there is no way of knowing – for more of the ordinary working people than ever before.

On the other hand, we must not fall into the trap of seeing nothing but misery and gloom in post-war Britain, even among the poor. As a result of the work of charitable religious societies, probably more poor children were now going to school than ever before. There were plenty of fair, even generous, employers and landlords. This was the time when Constable was able to paint the life of rustic England at its most attractive and satisfying.

There was no lack of speakers and writers eager to describe

vividly the wrongs of the poor and urge the means to right them. They demanded reform, *radical* reform. This expression, meaning reform that would get to the very root of the trouble, had been used in Parliament in the 1780s for relatively small matters, but now 'radicals' were those who wanted to go to the root of *all* the trouble in the country. They would reform Parliament, which would then be able to reform everything else – one radical leader called Spence hoped that it would nationalise land. Most radicals probably agreed with William Cobbett, ex-ploughman, ex-soldier, journalist. He edited a weekly paper, *The Political Register*, which cost two pence (2d.) and had a circulation of 50,000 by 1816. He demanded that every man should be given a vote in elections to Parliament, and wrote vehemently, furiously about what he considered to be injustices. But he was not a revolutionary, and would never tolerate violence.

Sometimes there were outbursts, though, perhaps because conditions seemed particularly desperate in a particular place, or because hot-heads took the lead. In 1816–17 there were riots in Cambridgeshire, London and Derbyshire, and a peaceful attempt at a march from Lancashire to London to ask for the help of the Prince Regent. These made the government imagine that bloody revolution would erupt if the authorities showed the slightest sign of weakness.

Crisis came in 1819. On 16 August a meeting was held at St Peter's Fields, Manchester, to hear the famous radical, 'Orator' Hunt. There was a crowd estimated at more than 50,000, perhaps very much more. The local magistrates feared that Hunt intended to stir the crowd up. They ordered the yeomanry cavalry to arrest Hunt, and a regular regiment to support the yeomanry. The crowd panicked, eleven were killed and hundreds hurt. The 'charge' was bitterly compared to the heroic deeds of only four years before, named 'Peterloo' and called a 'massacre' by the radicals. The government grew more alarmed than ever, and in December introduced 'The Six Acts' which radicals called oppressive. They

forbade people to drill and practise with weapons;

enabled magistrates to confiscate weapons;

restricted public meetings to 50 people, unless permitted by magistrates;

empowered magistrates to confiscate any writings they considered to be disloyal or blasphemous;

made weekly papers (like Cobbett's) more expensive by putting a stamp tax on them;

attempted to speed up trials by slightly restricting the rights of the defendant.

You must judge for yourself how far any or all of these acts were justified, but only two months later, in February 1820, something happened which seemed to show how real the danger was. A radical plot, called the Cato Street Conspiracy from the place where the plotters were discovered, aimed to murder leading members of the government.

In fact, the plot was a completely isolated case. Nothing like it occurred again. Soon afterwards trade began to improve, and gradually feelings became less intense.

The strain of enduring a long, hard war and the shock of adjusting to peace were over. Britain had come through victorious, richer and stronger than ever. Yet, looking back and recognising the forces that were at work, we can now see that old Britain was doomed. As the numbers of the people rose; as the old British traditions of liberty and law were given new vigour by ideas propagated by the French Revolution; as the people crowding to serve the ever-increasing machines came to understand their strength and opportunities; so it was bound to become obvious that the real source of power was the great body of ordinary people. The big questions would concern how they would claim that power, and who would claim to wield it in their name.

2 A revolutionary generation: Europe and Britain 1820−48

Romantics, rebels and reactionaries

Britain had borne a full part in Europe's struggle against France; in fact she had fought longer and more successfully than any of her allies. Yet, unlike the others, she had not really known war at first hand – the march of armies over the land, plunder, slaughter, destruction, the humiliation of being occupied, the ferocity of guerrilla fighting, the exultation of a defeated nation finally victorious over its erstwhile conqueror. The English Channel and the Royal Navy had insulated Britain from the fiercest passions of the warring Continent, and this may have made Britain less ready to accept violence as a way of deciding political disputes. But every part of Europe, no matter what particular circumstances and traditions affected it, belonged to the same civilisation and shared a common inheritance. They all were swayed by the development of new ideas, beliefs and fashions.

The first half of the nineteenth century was the age of the *Romantics*. As often happens, the new outlook showed very clearly in the art of the time. It was more emotional, dramatic, violent. Writers, painters and musicians felt that the old rules, the old forms of composition did not allow them to express their meaning fully, naturally and freely. Some of them went to absurd extremes and wallowed in emotion and fantasy; but the new freedom did allow great artists to create masterpieces which could not have been so powerful under the more restrained 'classical' styles of the old regime.

In music, this was the time of Beethoven and Schubert. Listen to them after hearing Bach and Handel, Mozart and Haydn. Was this a revolution? Another sort, perhaps, but as important as the French or the Industrial? Beethoven himself, living in imperial Vienna, was stirred by the noble and heroic appearance of France's wars in the name of liberty. He dedicated his Heroic (*Eroica*) Symphony to General

Ludwig van Beethoven, 1770–1827, drawn about 1818 by C. F. A. von Kloeber. A great musician who refused to give in to increasing deafness, he has often been taken as representing the heroic strength of the true Romantic artist.

below: A group of waltzers, depicted in 1819. The waltz could often be gay or sentimental – or both. It originated in German peasant dances.

Bonaparte, First Consul of the French Republic. But the Consul made himself Emperor, and Beethoven had to change his dedication – 'To the memory of a great man'.

In the ballroom the gavotte and minuet were swept aside by

The Lorelei rocks on the Rhine, painted by Myles Birkett Foster, 1825–99. The combination of legends and scenery in the Rhine valley attracted artists, poets and, as travel became easier, thousands of ordinary visitors.

'Rain, Steam and Speed – the Great Western Railway', painted in 1844 by J. M. W. Turner, 1775–1851. Thought by some to be the greatest of English painters, Turner delighted in the strength of colours, of natural forces and of man's creations.

the swirling waltz; it was, some thought, a regrettable sign of the times that waltzing couples held each other so closely.

In painting, a new violence appeared on canvas, both in the actions and the colours. Painters had a taste for the dramatic, and a fascinated interest in things that were mysterious and exotic, ruined and remote.

In literature, too, the appeal of 'far away and long ago' was irresistible, especially among the readers of novels. In the late eighteenth century some writers did a good trade in fantastic tales of horrors, of skeletons and ghosts in 'Gothick' castles and monasteries. This taste continued. In 1818 when she was 21 Mary Shelley, the poet's wife, published *Frankenstein*. The craze for historical novels really began in 1814 with the publication of *Waverley*. The author, Walter Scott, had already successfully published several long story–poems set in warlike olden times, with titles like *The Lay of the Last Minstrel* and *The Lady of the Lake*. Earlier still he had published a collection of traditional ballads, *Minstrelsy of the Scottish Border*, full of daring deeds and tragedy. After *Waverley* Scott went on to write stories ranging from the Middle Ages almost to his own time. He turned out dozens. The public seemed to have an insatiable appetite for romances of this sort, and other writers in many countries soon followed Scott. Most spectacular was Alexandre Dumas the Elder, who poured out novels and plays in hundreds; the most famous of all, *The Three Musketeers*, appeared in 1844.

Did the success of these colourful adventure-tales mean that the readers found their own lives tame and drab, and needed to escape into the imaginary world of the romances? Did it mean that there were many people who would want to behave like a Scott or Dumas character if ever they got the chance of excitement and action? Or did it mean merely that books were being made in great numbers and cheaply, and that there were more people to read them?

There was one typical fictional character whom it was fashionable to admire: the romantic hero, proud, disillusioned and often melancholy, sometimes heartless but capable of great and noble sacrifices. There was one man who seemed to be thus in real life; gifted, bitter, contemptuous of conventional society, he died in a war for liberty. He was Lord Byron. How far his manner and actions were natural, how far deliberately calculated to cause shock and sensation is something we cannot measure, but it does not matter very much. The important thing is that thousands of young men and women all over Europe believed in him. For many of them it was more than a fashion when they took up a Byronic pose. It was a sincere tribute to their hero and a gesture of defiance towards old-fashioned society.

The Romantic Movement in the arts was not a political movement. Many a composer, painter or writer was a perfectly peaceful subject of his government, a good number

left: *A page from the 1857 edition of Scott's 'The Lord of the Isles', first published in 1815.*

right: *George Gordon, Lord Byron, 1788–1824. A portrait of 1813 by Richard Westall.*

far right: *Clemens Wenzel Lothar, Prince Metternich-Winneburg, 1773–1859; lithograph from a portrait by F. Lieder. His influence was so strong that Liberals regarded him as the arch-oppressor of Europe.*

(like Scott himself) were strongly anti-revolutionary, and some earned riches, decorations and titles. As for the public who enjoyed hearing, seeing or reading Romantic works, they might hold any sort of opinion on politics – or no opinion at all. Nevertheless, a great number of the Romantics were in fact devoted to the ideal of liberty in Church and state as well as in the arts. To use a word which came to mean one of the great forces of the century, they believed in *liberalism*.

Liberals believed

> that people should be free to follow any religion or political party, profession or trade they thought fit,
>
> that the press should be free to print the truth as the journalists saw it,
>
> that all men should be treated fairly and that governments should be responsible to assemblies elected by their people as a whole.

This last point is where liberalism joined with another great force of the nineteenth century, *nationalism*. 'The people' may be the final source of power, but exactly who *are* they? How can 'the people' be defined, identified? The obvious answer seemed to be to include everybody belonging to a particular nation, which in practice generally meant

speaking that particular language. This simple commonsense definition, though, was only a small part of what a nationalist understood by the word 'nation'. For many centuries, and certainly since the rise of nation-states at the end of the Middle Ages, patriotism and national pride had often proved powerful in politics and war. A nationalist felt that his own people were the finest, the fairest, the bravest and best in the world. While liberalism meant liberty for all people, nationalism meant liberty for a particular people. The difference was to become a great deal more significant than it may sound.

The French Revolution had spread ideas of liberty all over Europe, and the French Empire had aroused national feelings against itself. The kings and aristocrats who regained control of Europe in 1815 after the final defeat of Napoleon were not fools. They saw clearly that such ideas and feelings could upset their intentions by making their subjects less docile and submissive. They wanted a return to the attitude of the old regime, with subjects dutifully obeying the authority of whatever legitimate king God had been pleased to place over them. The kings wished their peoples to settle quietly, so they agreed to work together to keep the peace. Every two or three years the chief statesmen of Europe would hold a congress, like the 1815 Congress of Vienna which succeeded in settling the map of Europe after the great wars. They would continue in the

Vienna spirit and settle disputes without fighting. It was an admirable idea, the first serious attempt ever made to preserve peace permanently among the great powers of Europe. Less practical, but well intentioned, Tsar Alexander I of Russia persuaded the kings of Europe to sign a Holy Alliance, declaring their intention to behave in a Christian spirit.

Unfortunately, the problem soon became how to ensure peace not *between* but *within* certain states. Had Congress statesmen any right to interfere inside other countries, even if invited by the kings of those countries? Most of them thought so. Guided by the Austrian Metternich, they believed that revolution in any country would spread to others if not quickly extinguished. Liberals thought of themselves as moving forward, making progress. Metternich and his friends were pushing back, *reacting* against progress. So anti-revolutionaries came to be called *reactionaries*.

The British government was reactionary like the others, and this seemed very true of Lord Castlereagh, the Foreign Secretary, who attended the Congresses. But there were deep differences between Britain and the other European monarchies, between parliamentary and despotic methods of government. The troubles of the 1820s would test how far the reactionary governments were prepared to go in asserting their peace, and how firmly they would hold to their principles when their own interests were involved.

The 1820 Revolutions and the interests of the Great Powers

The first crack in Congress Europe occurred early, in 1817, but could not be recognised as such at the time. The loser was the Turkish Empire, which was hardly considered as part of the European 'family', and the people who gained were the Christian Serbs, who had been encouraged in their revolt over several years by Russia. When the Serbs finally forced the Sultan to grant them self-government within his empire, the members of the Holy Alliance (under the influence of none other than the Tsar) were not worried. They could not recognise this as a warning of the increasing urgency of what came to be known as the Eastern Question, the explosive problem of what to do about Turkey and the Balkans. It was to vex everybody for the rest of the century and beyond.

The statesmen were more concerned about unrest among

the students in Germany. Little happened, apart from one dramatic assassination and a great deal of speech-making and singing, but Metternich took the opportunity to strengthen his influence and strengthen the police in the Germanic Confederation.

In 1820, the year of the Cato Street Conspiracy in Britain, revolt suddenly swept across southern Europe. Spain was first. In 1812 the leaders of the war against Napoleon had agreed that Spain ought to be ruled according to a liberal constitution. After the war, the king failed to honour this agreement. Now some liberal army officers took action. Colonel Riego seized power, and made the king promise to follow the constitution of 1812. Portugal was next. A rising began in Oporto, and a constitution was accepted in that monarchy too. In Italy, would-be revolutionaries were particularly fond of forming secret societies. The most widespread was that called the *Carbonari*, or Charcoal-burners. They began a revolt in what was probably the worst-governed state in Italy, Naples.

During 1821 revolts spread. There was a rising in the principalities of Wallachia and Moldavia (later to be called Romania) which was meant to spark off another rising among the Greek subjects of Turkey. A few months later Greeks in the Morea (southern Greece) did rise, and they massacred the Turks living amongst them. Meanwhile the Carbonari set off another rising, this time in Piedmont at the other end of Italy from Naples. The news from South America, too, was likely to hearten anyone thinking of revolution, for here the Spanish colonies, after years of confusion and bitter fighting, were now obviously winning their independence.

The statesmen met at the Congresses of Troppau, Laibach and Verona. All of the 'Big Five' – Austria, Russia, Prussia, France, Britain – agreed that the situation was dangerous, but they did not agree on what action to take. Austria, Russia and Prussia thought it best to march troops into any country suffering from an outbreak of revolution, so as to stop the disease in its early stages. Britain thought that what went on inside a country was that country's own business, and that there was nothing wrong in setting up a constitution with a parliament; therefore other armies should interfere only if a revolution definitely threatened the peace of neighbouring states. France usually preferred the British attitude.

It was not merely a difference of theories, however. Austria was directly involved because she held part of Italy. In 1821, with the approval of most of the Congress of Laibach, Austria sent troops into Naples and Piedmont, and put down the revolutions in both kingdoms. France, whatever her usual attitude to interfering may have been in principle, was in practice worried about what was going on just across the frontier, in Spain. In 1822, with the approval this time of most of the Congress of Verona, France sent troops into Spain and overthrew Riego. There was one astonishing thing about this invasion; most Spaniards welcomed the French. Yet it was less than ten years since a great number of the Spanish people had been fighting with relentless ferocity to drive the French from the Peninsula. The reason was that then the French had been trying to change Spain, remove the king and weaken the Church; this time, on the contrary, they were rescuing king and Church from Riego and his liberals. It is important to remember that, whatever they may have claimed in their speeches and newspapers, revolutionaries did not always want what most of the people wanted.

Now, having restored royal power in Spain, should the Congress go on to do the same in the Spanish American colonies? At this point Britain stepped in, and made it plain that the Royal Navy would be ordered to prevent any Congress troops from landing in South America. There could be no argument with the mistress of the sea. President Monroe of the U.S.A. took the opportunity to declare that his country would never permit foreign interference in any part of the New World; this has become known as the Monroe Doctrine, and at the time it seemed empty words, since the U.S.A. was powerless to stop any invasion. But why was Britain so interested? Partly, no doubt, because she distrusted the despotic powers, but also because South America was already becoming a very good market for the products of the British Industrial Revolution. After this, though the Powers remained on friendly terms and consulted one another about international problems, there were no more congresses.

There was still the Greek revolt. The Turkish government soon suppressed the original Romanian rising, but found mountainous Greece far tougher. Many of the Greek 'patriots' had lived as bandits, or pirates among the islands, and saw the revolt as a splendid chance to extend their brutal trades. The Turks were not slow to retaliate, and hanged the Patriarch of the Greek Church, who lived in Constantinople and had nothing to do with the slaughter. The Greeks took the Turkish stronghold of Tripolitsa, and massacred 10,000 people. The Turks took the Greek island of Chios and massacred or enslaved most of the inhabitants. The Greek rebels were often crippled by feuds between their leaders, but the Sultan did not dare to withdraw enough good troops from other parts of his empire to crush the revolt. However, there was an efficient army and navy in Egypt, which was officially part of the Turkish Empire, though the Viceroy of Egypt, Mehemet Ali, in fact behaved more like an independent king. The Sultan persuaded him to help, and when the Egyptian forces invaded Greece in 1825 it looked as if the rebellion was as good as finished.

Could Europe allow the Greeks to go under? Now the

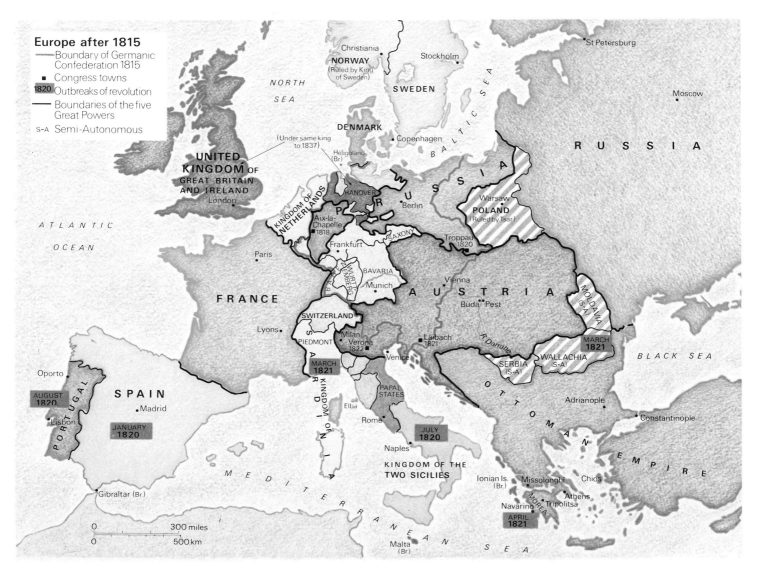

Europe after 1815

Boundary of Germanic Confederation 1815

■ Congress towns

1820 Outbreaks of revolution

Boundaries of the five Great Powers

S-A Semi-Autonomous

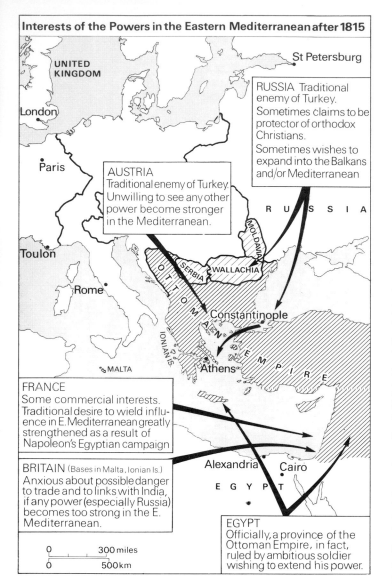

Interests of the Powers in the Eastern Mediterranean after 1815

UNITED KINGDOM

London

St Petersburg

RUSSIA Traditional enemy of Turkey. Sometimes claims to be protector of orthodox Christians. Sometimes wishes to expand into the Balkans and/or Mediterranean

Paris

AUSTRIA Traditional enemy of Turkey. Unwilling to see any other power become stronger in the Mediterranean.

RUSSIA

MOLDAVIA

Toulon

SERBIA

WALLACHIA

Rome

OTTOMAN

Constantinople

IONIANS

EMPIRE

MALTA

Athens

FRANCE Some commercial interests. Traditional desire to wield influence in E. Mediterranean greatly strengthened as a result of Napoleon's Egyptian campaign

BRITAIN (Bases in Malta, Ionian Is.) Anxious about possible danger to trade and to links with India, if any power (especially Russia) becomes too strong in the E. Mediterranean.

Alexandria Cairo

EGYPT

EGYPT Officially, a province of the Ottoman Empire, in fact, ruled by ambitious soldier wishing to extend his power.

0   300 miles

0   500 km

question was urgent, and a strong feeling spread among educated people everywhere that the home of classical civilisation must not perish in flames and blood. Even if modern Greeks did not seem to resemble their illustrious forefathers very closely, they were still the heirs of Leonidas and Pericles, and civilised Europeans felt that there was a debt to be honoured. Even if it meant helping rebels and inter-

fering inside another state, Greece must be saved. Already volunteers had gone to help the Greeks, and among them was Byron. In the besieged fortress of Missolonghi he died of fever in 1824, and to Romantics this gave an added glamour to the cause of Greek liberty.

Ironically, the power most likely to come to the aid of the Greek rebels was the most reactionary of all – Russia. Many of the Tsar's ministers saw this as a chance to weaken the traditional enemy, Turkey, and to increase Russian influence in the Middle East. Russia already claimed to have a special right to protect all the Christian subjects of the Sultan. The prospect of Russia acting on her own and increasing her strength did not please the other powers, and they combined to persuade her to be patient while negotiations were tried. First Britain and Russia together tried to stand between Turks and Greeks, diplomatically speaking, and argue both sides into a settlement. Then France joined them, and all three sent warships to the Greek coast, to emphasise their arguments for a truce and a peace. The result was misunderstanding, distrust, and on 20 October 1827 the combined British–Russian–French fleet attacked and destroyed the Egyptian fleet at Navarino, near where, in other centuries, Actium and Lepanto had been fought. After this Mehemet Ali realised that the European powers would never allow him to succeed, and in 1828 accepted a French offer to ferry the Egyptian army home. Still the Sultan would not give way and Russia, despite British disapproval, declared war on Turkey.

Russia herself had not been entirely free from revolutionary troubles. At the end of 1825 a group of liberal army officers in St Petersburg tried to seize power. They are known as the Decembrists. Within twenty-four hours they had all been arrested, and were hanged or exiled. It had not been a serious threat. The Russian state may often have seemed inefficient and corrupt, but it showed gigantic strength. When the Tsar's armies moved against Turkey they bore down dogged Turkish resistance, took forts and passes, and by August 1829 reached Adrianople. The Sultan admitted defeat.

Meanwhile the statesmen of Britain, France and Russia had been meeting in London to decide what frontiers a new Greek state ought to have. In September 1829, by the Treaty of Adrianople, Turkey accepted what the allies had decided, and Greece, though still supposed to be vaguely under the Sultan's influence, became self-governing. As for Russia, she

Makriyannis (Big John), a Greek rebel leader; lithograph from a sketch made by K. Krazeisen in 1828. Born in 1797, he survived many desperate battles, severe wounds and the murderous rivalry of other rebel leaders to become a general after independence, to be a prominent politician, to write his memoirs and to die peacefully in 1864.

Charles X; born 1757, king 1824, deposed 1830, died 1836. This portrait by J. A. D. Ingres, 1780–1867, was painted in 1829 and emphasises the sacred dignity of kingship.

was given compensation for her efforts and expenses. Russia was not greedy, made no big demands. She had been victorious and was in a strong position for the next move.

As the decade ended, only one European revolt of the 1820s had achieved success, and it was truly the exception that proves the rule. The Greek revolt was on the outer fringe of Europe, and was against a government which had for centuries been regarded as a dangerous alien by other European governments. It was not a rising of new-fashioned liberals and nationalists, but more like another bloody episode in the old feud of Cross and Crescent – and some saw it as older still, the fight of West against East which the Greeks had been sustaining since the days of Marathon and Salamis. This, surely, was such an exceptional case that it could never be taken as encouraging liberal revolutionary movements in the rest of Europe, nor as a failure of reactionary governments. Indeed, those very governments had saved the rebels. The most important reason for the success of the Greek revolt is probably that it was in the interests of certain great powers that it should succeed.

The 1830 Revolutions

Historians have tended to label 1830 as the first big 'year of revolutions' of the nineteenth century, possibly because those of 1820 failed, probably because those of 1830 occurred nearer the centres of European power. Since 1789 Paris had been thought of as the home of revolution; in 1820 it had been quiet, but in 1830 the troubles began in Paris.

Fifteen years earlier, the Bourbon royal family had been brought back by the victorious Allies. The Bourbons, it was said, learned nothing and forgot nothing. Certainly, many royalists wanted to avenge everything they had suffered, and to rule France as if the previous quarter-century of Revolution and Empire had never happened. But the king, Louis XVIII, knew well enough that it was impossible to undo history, and he was willing to be a constitutional king. There was a written constitution, known as the Charter, and a Chamber of Deputies rather like the British House of Commons. Probably none of the main political parties, whether royalist or Bonapartist or republican, thought that the Charter was good, but they put up with it. After so many years of change and war, Frenchmen accepted the Charter as a reasonable compromise, as long as they had an easy-going king who was content to jog peacefully along.

Louis XVIII died in 1824 and was succeeded by his brother, Charles X. It was a little like Britain in 1685, when a shrewd, realistic king was replaced by a bigoted brother. The new king began by compensating nobles who had lost land in the Revolution, at the expense of the taxpayers. He tried to restore

left: 'Liberty leading the People', a romantic view of the Paris revolution painted in 1830 by Eugene Delacroix, 1798–1863. The man in the top hat is said to be the artist. The new government rewarded him by making him a member of the Legion of Honour.

right: A photograph of Louis Philippe in 1845.

to the Church its old wealth and power, even making some forms of sacrilege punishable by death. He disbanded the National Guard, the part-time defence force which had been set up in 1789 and which the middle class had always regarded as their own, their protection against tyranny on the one hand and mob violence on the other. Because most of the Chamber of Deputies disapproved, Charles appointed a prime minister and government who would obey him, the king, rather than the Chamber. He seems to have believed that he was quite secure, but in any case a successful foreign war would rouse the French to patriotic enthusiasm for their victorious king. In June 1830 French troops attacked the old pirate city of Algiers and began the conquest of Algeria. On 26 July the king dissolved the Chamber of Deputies, altered the Charter so that new elections would favour his supporters, and ordered hostile newspapers to cease publication. Now, he thought, he had the power to be a real king. But he had miscalculated.

That same day a liberal writer named Adolphe Thiers issued a protest on behalf of the journalists of Paris; the banned newspapers refused to be suppressed, and were published as usual. The Chamber of Deputies refused to be dissolved, and met and protested. So far, only words. On 28 July came action. Rebels built barricades across many of the streets, and occupied the Town Hall. Soldiers made only half-

hearted attempts to stop them, and it was this unwillingness of the army to support the king that decided the revolt. On 1 August the king fled to England.

It happened astonishingly quickly, easily – and entirely in Paris. At the barricades there had been young romantics, many of them artists and writers, but the men who now decided the future of France were old and experienced. One was Talleyrand, a bishop before 1789, whose smooth cunning had kept him in positions of influence under almost every government since. Another was Lafayette, the marquis who had fought beside Washington for American independence, had been the first commander of the National Guard, and now emerged from retirement, a venerable link with those days of heroic legend. Many liberals wanted France to be a republic again, with old Lafayette as president, but most of the Chamber of Deputies thought it safer to stick to constitutional monarchy, if they could find a sincerely constitutional king. They found one in Louis Philippe, Duke of Orleans. His father, though a royal prince, had become a revolutionary in the 1790s and had voted for the execution of Louis XVI, while Louis Philippe himself as a young man had served in the Revolutionary army. Now he was a staid, middle-aged moderate – a 'safe' choice.

So began what is known as the July Monarchy, or the

Orleans Monarchy. Louis Philippe has also been called 'the bourgeois king' because he looked and behaved like a prosperous middle-class merchant. The July Revolution turned out to have been a very mild one indeed; it was not really a revolution at all, but the replacement of an unco-operative constitutional king by a willing one. During the next few years there were violent outbursts by disappointed republicans, particularly in Lyons and Paris. But the news that sped across Europe in the late summer of 1830 was only that there had been a successful revolt in Paris and that liberals now ruled France.

The Kingdom of the Netherlands was artificial, erected in 1815 by the Congress statesmen to act as a barrier against any renewed revolutionary or imperialist adventures from France. The southern Netherlands, sometimes called Belgium after the Belgae who had dwelt there in Roman times, had remained

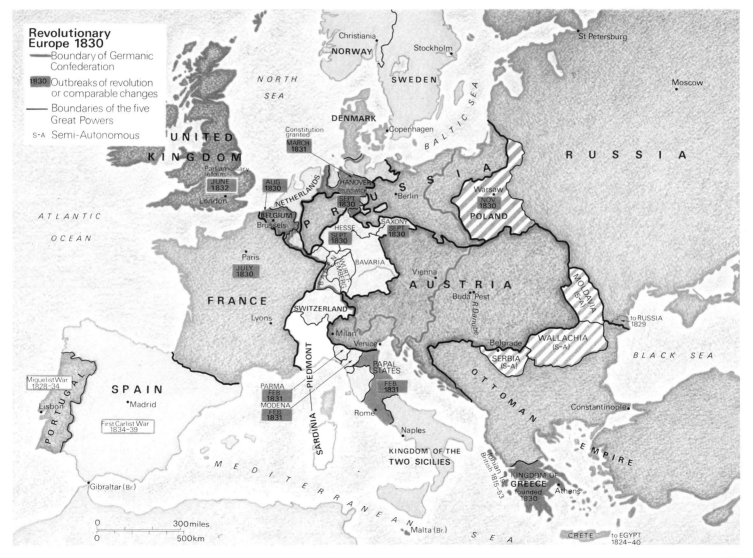

under the Habsburgs when the northern Netherlands, or United Provinces, had won their independence from Spain two centuries before. The Belgians may not have been one identical mass, but almost all of them were Catholics, and spoke either French or Flemish. They had not wanted to be placed under a king of the Dutch House of Orange, and still resented being treated merely as part of his kingdom. In August 1830, encouraged by the news from Paris, a deputation claiming to represent all Belgians visited the king and asked him to grant Belgium self-government. The king took this as a challenge to his authority, and refused to discuss the matter until his troops had seized control of Brussels. It was a bad miscalculation. Street fighting broke out, the Dutch troops withdrew, there were risings all over Belgium and a national congress met in November. The congress declared that Belgium was an independent kingdom and there was no reason why its king should belong to the House of Orange.

Surprised and humiliated, the Dutch king appealed to the great powers that had guaranteed the Vienna settlement. Unluckily for him, Austria, Russia and Prussia were very concerned at the time with Poland and Italy, and anyway the Belgians did not sound too terribly revolutionary if all they wanted was another king. So the three powers which might have taken firm action did nothing. That left Britain and France. Both were near enough to intervene easily, but neither of these governments would force the Belgians back under Dutch rule. So eventually the powers agreed that Belgium should be independent, and must always remain not only independent but also neutral. It was well known that the French hoped that some day Belgium would be joined to France, as it had been for the twenty years before 1814, and the other powers had no intention of letting anything so dangerous happen. The Belgians were forbidden to choose a French prince as their king, and in June 1831 they offered the new crown to Leopold of Saxe-Coburg, a German prince then living in England. Furious, the Dutch king tried to regain Belgium by force, but the arrival of French troops and British warships forced him at last to accept his loss.

Leopold had a reputation for brains. He proved to be a clever ruler, and Belgium prospered. It has been said that in 1830 it was doubtful if such a thing as a Belgian nation existed, but there was no doubt when the nineteenth century ended.

While a new nation was coming to life in western Europe, an old one was struggling for freedom in eastern Europe. The Vienna settlement had restored the Kingdom of Poland, though leaving some of its former territories in the hands of Austria and Prussia. The King of Poland, though, was to be none other than the Tsar of Russia. It is true that he promised to treat Poland as a separate country, with its own constitution and laws, church and army, and that on the whole he kept his word. But the Polish Parliament was hardly ever consulted and the Polish nobility, ever independent, brave and quarrelsome, bitterly resented being subject to their despised traditional enemies, the uncouth Muscovites. Secret societies throve, pledged to throw off Russian rule. This feeling could not be concealed from the Tsar and his ministers, and they planned to strengthen their grip and suppress the Polish constitution.

As news of successful revolts arrived from Paris and then Brussels, excitement mounted. Tension tightened when a rumour spread that the Tsar intended to send Polish troops to put down the people of Paris and Brussels. A mob in Warsaw attacked the palace of the Russian viceroy, who happened to be a brother of the Tsar. Shocked, he fled from Poland in November, taking all his Russian regiments with him. Leading Poles set up a government and declared that the Tsar was no longer their king. It looked as though yet another revolution in 1830 had succeeded with astonishing speed and ease.

This revolution, however, was dealing with the most powerful autocrat in the world. In the spring of 1831 Russian armies moved into Poland. The Polish army fought with its traditional dash, but the sheer size of the Russian forces

Frederic Chopin, 1810–49, sketched by Delacroix. Though his father was French and he lived in Paris from 1831, Chopin brought Polish nationalism into concert music with his mazurkas and polonaises.

crushed all resistance. By autumn the Tsar again ruled in Warsaw, and now there was no attempt to treat Poland as a separate country. Poland became simply another province of the Russian Empire, held in an iron grip.

In western Europe there was sympathy for the Poles. They appealed to the imagination of Romantics. They were recklessly heroic, unlucky and unhappy, and some of them – the best known – were brilliant and handsome. To many, the music and the long losing struggle against illness of Frederic Chopin summed up the sad tale of Poland.

In Italy the Carbonari did not manage to organise risings until February 1831. Their intention was to sweep the whole of northern Italy, but revolts materialised only in the Duchies of Parma and Modena, and in the Papal States. Within a few weeks the Austrian army stamped them out. It was becoming obvious that the secret societies were a fiasco, and a young would-be revolutionary named Giuseppe Mazzini tried to build up instead one national political movement, Young Italy. But this turned out to have no more luck than the old societies. Mazzini and his friends planned rising after rising. Every time their plans were discovered or the revolts fell flat.

In Germany, some of the princes in a few of the smaller states were forced or persuaded to grant constitutions. There was a good deal of revolutionary talk, but little action.

So the 1830 wave of revolutions died away. Four areas had been greatly affected, and in two of them the revolutions had succeeded. Were they part of a general European revolutionary feeling which was getting hold of the people of the continent as a whole? Certainly the spark from Paris had lit fuel in many places, but was it really the same sort of fuel? There were great differences in the reasons behind the revolts, in the amount of fighting that took place, in the circumstances which led to success or failure. We could question whether they were all genuine revolutions, whether they were led by liberals, or nationalists, or both, or neither. Above all we can ask what the bulk of the people did. Did they rise spontaneously, all together? Did they do as they were told? Did they mostly look on, while others claimed to be acting for them?

In the end, who or what decided whether the rising succeeded or failed? In other words, where did the power really reside?

In Britain: reform from above

It may seem that Britain's problems, though different, were just as serious as those of the countries where risings took place. Over the past few decades there had been no lack of ideas on how the government ought to try to seek solutions.

Jeremy Bentham (1748–1832) was the most famous British political writer of his time, throughout Europe and America as well as Britain. He was a man of enormous intellect; at the age of three he had read Rapin's *History of England* and begun to learn Latin, and his powers did not flag during the rest of his long life. His greatest interest was in law and ethics, in how people ought to behave towards one another. The guiding principle, in his eyes, should be 'the greatest happiness of the greatest number'. He would test laws – and anything else – by how useful they were towards this happiness, and therefore called his belief *utilitarianism*. (He ordered that when he died, in order to be of more use, his body should be dissected and his skeleton preserved and exhibited in University College, London; it still dwells there.)

Bentham's ideals were generous and helpful, but would conditions allow them to work? Thomas Malthus (1766–1834) had been brought up among people who admired the eloquent but non-practical teachings of Rousseau. Partly to show the difficulties that these optimists tended to ignore, he argued in his *Essay on Population* (1798) that a growing population naturally increases faster than its food supplies, and the greatest care is needed to prevent poverty and want from becoming worse. Some people misinterpreted his theory as meaning that nothing could prevent the miseries of the poor and that the wealthy should not feel responsible.

There were others who appeared to believe that there were laws of economics, of finance and business which people were bound to follow if they wished to prosper. David Ricardo (1772–1823), a very successful financier, published his *Principles of Political Economy and Taxation* in 1817, and among his theories was the idea that higher wages meant lower profits, and vice versa (though he did not say that higher wages automatically caused prices to rise). If such ideas were correct, employers and employees must always be opposed.

There were many theories to choose from, but William Huskisson, President of the Board of Trade in the 1820s, held to the ideas of Adam Smith (page 20). He began once more to reduce tariffs, and he relaxed the Navigation Acts which dated from the seventeenth century when, according to the mercantile theory of trade, foreign ships and merchants had to be kept away from British colonies. At first some British manufacturers feared that their protection was being removed and that foreign competition would overwhelm them. They were mistaken. Trade boomed in the earlier 1820s, and Britain's Industrial Revolution had put her far ahead in many industries, which had a great advantage wherever trade was free.

Meanwhile the Revolution was going on, with more machines, some new and some improved; more factories and mines; more workers and streets of cheap houses. These things were gradually altering the appearance of Britain. The most obvious sign of all this change was the railway.

The problem of putting steam on the roads was solved by building special roads, with rails. Wagon-ways had long been used on the North-Eastern Coalfield to move loads of coal from the mines to the barges and ships. Stationary steam engines were introduced to haul trains of wagons, hitched to a cable, up slopes. Finally, in 1813 William Hedley built *Puffing Billy,* a locomotive whose smooth iron wheels ran on smooth iron rails without slipping. In 1825 the Stockton and Darlington Railway was opened, mainly to carry coal but also usable for other goods and for passengers. When this proved a success, a railway was planned between the port of Liverpool and the cotton capital of Manchester. As with turnpikes and canals, Parliament had to give permission, and this time there were strong objections. Some people disliked the idea of iron tracks cutting across the countryside, carrying noisy, dirty machines. Some worried about the effect on passengers; would flesh and blood, nerve and brain endure the strain of being hurled through the air at thirty miles an hour? Such was the speed claimed for George Stephenson's *Rocket,* the locomotive which won the contest for the best engine to work the new railway. But objections and difficulties were overcome, and the line was opened in 1830. Huskisson was a guest of honour at the opening. Apparently confused by the noise and excitement, he stepped in front of the locomotive and was fatally injured, the first known victim of a railway accident.

If any one thing were to be taken as the symbol of the nineteenth century, summing up the changes, it would have to be the railway. Within a couple of decades there was a network of rails across Britain; in the 1840s the rush to build was rightly

nicknamed 'the railway mania'. Transport of goods and people became unbelievably fast and cheap – unbelievable, that is, to men and women who had never known anything faster than a coach drawn by horses. Other European countries were eager to share the benefits. Railways began in France, 1828; Austria, 1828; Russia, 1833; Germany, 1835; Italy, 1840; Spain, 1848; Turkey, 1860. Soon railways crossed all continents. By the end of the century there were over half a million miles of railway track throughout the world, about 180,000 miles of them in Europe and 200,000 in the U.S.A.

Despite its suspicion of radicals and would-be revolutionaries, the British government in the 1820s could be persuaded that some changes in the laws were now necessary and right. After Huskisson had begun to free trade, even the Corn Laws were eased; a 'sliding scale' was substituted for the fixed tariff. The Combination Acts were repealed, so that trade unions, under certain limits, were permitted. Most remarkable of all was the reform of the criminal laws and the police which was effected by the Home Secretary, Sir Robert Peel.

Peel's own background was an example of how changes were taking place in the ruling classes themselves. His grandfather, of farming stock, had taken to clothmaking and employed Hargreaves. His father, the first Sir Robert Peel, a very wealthy man, had in 1802 persuaded Parliament to pass the first Factory Act, protecting apprentices. (It ordered that they should not work more than twelve hours per day.)

The Home Secretary looked at the criminal law of England and concluded that it was not working. It was too severe. Over the previous century a huge number of offences had been made punishable by hanging or transportation. There was often in practice no difference between the penalty for murder and for petty theft. As a result, juries sometimes preferred to acquit a guilty man rather than send him to death or exile for a minor crime. Therefore Peel began to make sweeping reductions in punishments, a policy continued by later governments.

At the same time he realised that the first thing was to *catch* the culprits. Crime was worst in the big cities, so he began with the biggest, London. The Metropolitan Police Act of 1829 made the Home Secretary directly responsible for order in the capital, with power to employ a police force. At first many people distrusted the idea. They feared that the government would use the force as many European governments used their police — to suppress critics and protesters. But Peel was determined that this would not happen. His men would not be at all like soldiers; they were civilians, unarmed except for a stick. It worked. Within a few years the local authorities in other cities and counties set up similar police forces, and in 1856 Parliament made it compulsory for every county to have its own force. Before the century ended, the British 'bobbies' were trusted and liked by most of the people they controlled and protected.

Nobody could deny that these were serious attempts to improve conditions in different ways. But these reforms were not big enough and quick enough to satisfy large numbers of people. There were fresh outbursts of discontent.

It may seem odd, but the issue that aroused most excitement in the late 1820s was a very old one, going back to the passions and persecutions of Tudor and Stuart times. Religious penal laws that had been passed then were still on the statute book. Though it was a long time since Catholics had been fined for not attending the Church of England, and though they quietly held their own services with their own priests, they still lacked some rights. Catholics could not be M.P.s, magistrates, town councillors, navy or army officers. Many people thought that it was absurd to carry on this system, and that Catholics should be freed, or *emancipated*. Many Protestants, however, thought that this would be a betrayal of their religion. Several attempts in Parliament since 1801 to help the Catholics had failed, though sometimes they had passed the House of Commons but not the Lords.

In most parts of Britain, Catholics were too few to cause much of a problem, but it was different in Ireland. Most of the Irish people were Catholics, and they had plenty of injustice and oppression to complain about. In 1800 Ireland's Parliament had been united with that which represented the rest of Britain—it was then that St Patrick's Cross was added to the British flag—and Irish M.P.s now sat at Westminster. It seemed to a Catholic Irish lawyer named Daniel O'Connell that the first step towards getting better treatment for his people was to get some Irish Catholic M.P.s. Therefore in 1828 O'Connell himself stood as candidate in County Clare, and was elected by a huge majority. Parliament refused to accept him. The electors refused to elect anyone else. It was stalemate.

Contemporary cartoons give opposite views on Catholic Emancipation. In one, Wellington and Peel are shown as the recently tried Edinburgh murderers, Burke and Hare, killing Mrs Constitution (born 1688) in order to sell the corpse; in this case the surgeon coming to buy the body is a Catholic priest. The other cartoon shows Wellington and Peel discussing the folly of their opponents, thrown into a panic by a make-believe monster.

So far all had gone quietly. The peace and order were astonishing. But could this last? The Irish were determined. It was only thirty years since a great armed rebellion, and there had been plots since, and executions. The man who must decide, the Prime Minister, happened to be the most famous

37

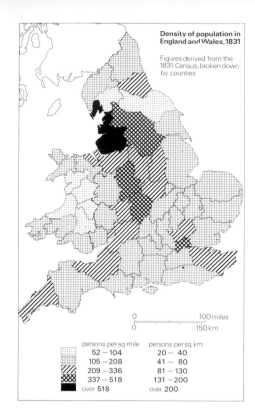

Density of population in
England and Wales, 1831

Figures derived from the
1831 Census, broken down
by counties

	0	100 miles
	0	150 km

	persons per sq mile	persons per sq km
	52 — 104	20 — 40
	105 — 208	41 — 80
	209 — 336	81 — 130
	337 — 518	131 — 200
	over 518	over 200

soldier alive, the 'Iron Duke' himself. Wellington saw no good reason for Catholic emancipation. On the other hand, he had seen enough of war not to want to risk a civil war in Ireland. It was simply not worth fighting over this issue. Fortunately, Wellington was strong enough to be able to make the other Tories accept his decision. With the Catholic Emancipation Act of 1829, giving Catholics virtually the same rights as their Protestant fellow-citizens, it seemed that the centuries of religious intolerance in Britain were coming to an end.

Though the crisis had been about Catholics, and especially in Ireland, there were many thousands of Protestants in England and Wales who had also suffered under the old acts because they did not belong to the Church of England. Some were descended from seventeenth-century Puritan sects, but the most powerful were the Methodists, founded by the Wesley brothers in the eighteenth century. These had a huge following in the industrial towns and villages. The Protestant Nonconformists, as such people were called, had a strong tradition of respecting hard work and plain practical morality, and of being unimpressed by inherited rank and privileges. They were not violent, not revolutionaries, but they always put their considerable weight behind proposals for reform. Religion was certainly not ceasing to be a force in British life. On the contrary, it seemed to grow stronger as the century developed, and some historians have seen the 'Nonconformist conscience' as responsible for much of the effort and achievement.

The problems of poverty remained untouched meanwhile, and from time to time some of the poor could endure their lot no longer. In 1830 and 1831 riots broke out across the southern counties of England. They were not a response to revolutionary inspiration from Paris. They arose from the desperate resentment of farm workers who for many years had been paid at bare subsistence level, who were treated sometimes with humiliating harshness by insolent employers, who knew of the talk of change and improvement but could see no prospects of better treatment for themselves. These were the people who had not gained from the Agricultural Revolution, just as their relatives who had migrated to the towns had often done badly from the Industrial Revolution.

Parliament, stuffed with landowners, their friends and their clients, seemed unwilling or unable to interfere with conditions in either the countryside or the towns. To those people who wanted something done about the problems, it was becoming obvious that the first problem was Parliament itself. The House of Commons would have to be reformed.

It was easy to find fault with the system of electing M.P.s in 1830. To anybody who thought that it should be a simple matter of counting heads, the system was a bad joke. Some towns had dwindled but still had M.P.s. Old Sarum, no longer even a village, was the most notorious example, but there were other 'rotten' boroughs, some in the 'pocket' of a powerful landowner. Corruption was not so flagrant as it had been in the time of Sir Robert Walpole, but there was still a great deal. Many a seat was permanently controlled by one group. Where elections took place, bribery and threats were often used. Yet despite a rivalry between Tories and Whigs that was often bitter, the candidates were in fact usually the same sort of people: wealthy men, gentlemen, friends of peers. Very rarely a man with radical ideas was elected M.P. Generally the system was that the upper classes controlled Parliament and ruled Britain.

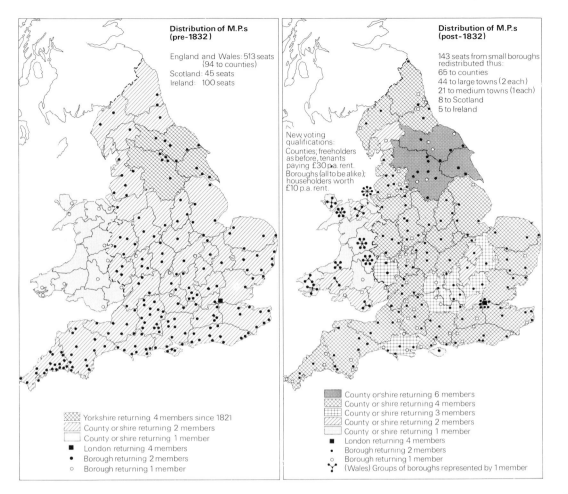

Distribution of M.P.s
(pre-1832)

England and Wales: 513 seats
(94 to counties)
Scotland: 45 seats
Ireland: 100 seats

Distribution of M.P.s
(post-1832)

143 seats from small boroughs
redistributed thus:
65 to counties
44 to large towns (2 each)
21 to medium towns (1 each)
8 to Scotland
5 to Ireland

New voting
qualifications:
Counties; freeholders
as before, tenants
paying £30 p.a. rent.
Boroughs (all to be alike);
householders worth
£10 p.a. rent.

Yorkshire returning 4 members since 1821
County or shire returning 2 members
County or shire returning 1 member
■ London returning 4 members
● Borough returning 2 members
○ Borough returning 1 member

County or shire returning 6 members
County or shire returning 4 members
County or shire returning 3 members
County or shire returning 2 members
County or shire returning 1 member
■ London returning 4 members
● Borough returning 2 members
○ Borough returning 1 member
⅄ (Wales) Groups of boroughs represented by 1 member

Even among these there were many M.P.s who thought that seats were unfairly distributed among the towns and counties, and there had been attempts at reform (page 20). Others, however, especially among the Tories, produced strong arguments for retaining the system as it was.

Firstly, it worked. For more than a century Britain had been growing richer and stronger, had an unequalled record of victory in war, and had been recognised as the most free and tolerant of all the great powers. A system which produced such results was too good to be changed.

Secondly, an M.P. did not represent only the people who voted him in. His duty was to consider what was good for the whole of Britain and her empire. So it was a mistake to argue that the people of the industrial areas were not represented – just as the American colonists' slogan of 'No taxation without representation' had been mistaken.

Thirdly, the system was not based on simple head-counting. All men were not equal. The system tried to ensure that men of experience and wisdom, education and culture, men accustomed to the responsibility of handling property and instructing others, would rule the country. It would be folly to hand over power to the ignorant and inexperienced. Even the 'rotten' boroughs had a good use; it sometimes happened that a wise man who would be valuable in the Commons was unable to fight an ordinary election, but he could be given a safe seat like Old Sarum.

The radicals, who were not impressed by such arguments, had never ceased to speak and write for a reform of Parliament. By 1830 they had convinced most of the ordinary people, and also the Whig peers and gentlemen who sat in the Houses of Lords and Commons. These Whigs had been kept out of power for about two generations. It might be possible, they thought, to make the Commons more broadly based and thus out-number their Tory opponents without making a revolutionary change. In November 1830 the Tory government was defeated in a vote in the House of Commons. It was apparently an unimportant matter, but the Duke of Wellington realised that it showed that the House no longer supported him, so he resigned. The Whig leader, Earl Grey, became Prime Minister.

In March 1831 Grey's government introduced a Bill for the Reform of Parliament. It just failed to get through the Commons. Grey asked the king to dissolve Parliament, and there was a general election amidst great excitement. Though most ordinary people had no vote, it was also true that many voters in counties and some boroughs were quite poor. Also, there was no doubt that most people in Britain were in favour of reform, including many wealthy people. Even the farmers seemed to have lost faith in their Tory protectors, and voted Whig. So the Whigs came back with a big majority, and this time their Reform Bill passed the Commons easily. Now the House of Lords rejected it. There were riots in Bristol and Nottingham, where the castle was burned down.

Neither side would give way. Earl Grey proved to be the only possible Prime Minister, because he had most of the Commons behind him. Wellington, leading a big Tory majority in the Lords, stood just as firmly against any weakening (as he regarded it) of the British constitution. The deadlock ended when the king gave way. Pressed by Grey, William IV finally consented to create enough new Whig peers to out-vote the Tories in the House of Lords. This threat was decisive. Wellington knew when he was beaten. When the Reform Bill next came before the House of Lords, Wellington and the Tory lords walked out, and left the Whig lords to pass it.

You must have noticed that, no matter how noisy or strong the popular demand for the Reform Act may have been, the real battle was fought out between the aristocratic leaders of the two great parties. The victors were no more ordinary people than their opponents were; they were lords and gentlemen. But they, the Whigs, were now in power for the first time in decades. The price they had paid for their victory was to admit others to share power with them. But these others were not the mass of ordinary people, only a limited number of the reasonably well-off. The Whigs intended this to be the limit. It was all right to extend the franchise among the middle classes, but never to the uneducated, irresponsible masses.

This does not mean that the Whigs were against making things better. They intended to stop cruelty, injustice and corruption. While they were in power Parliament passed several reforms. In 1833 the long agitation against slavery finally succeeded, and all slaves throughout the British Empire were set free. That same year, a new Factory Act reduced the hours that women and 'young persons' (under 18) could work to 10 per day; children (9–13) to 8 per day; and forbade those under 9 to be employed at all. What was more, inspectors were appointed to enforce the law, and in 1836 the compulsory registration of births, marriages and deaths helped to make it easier to check ages. In 1833 the government granted £20,000 to help the religious and charitable societies which were providing elementary education for increasing numbers of children; it was not much, but it was the first time that a British government (unlike some enlightened European governments of the past century) had shown any sign of thinking it might have a duty to educate its subjects. The idea was to grow with astonishing speed. In 1835 town councils were cleaned up. The

Inside a spinning factory, 1835.

Municipal Corporations Act ordered that councils should be properly elected by all the taxpayers, and thus replaced all the old town charters which had enabled little groups of local bigwigs to run boroughs entirely as they wished.

As far as they went, these acts were honest attempts to make life better. The claim that the British government was concerned more about black slaves on West Indian plantations than white slaves in farms, factories and mines nearer home was not fair. However, Parliament was not soft. The 1834 Poor Law Amendment Act is probably the best example of their attitude. Under the old Poor Law and the Speenhamland system (page 21), unemployed and underpaid people got money from local taxes to keep them going. The cost of this outdoor relief, as it was called, was very high. It was suspected that many employers paid their workers less than living wages, though they could have afforded them, because they knew that the taxes would always make up the difference. Worse still, the workers were being demoralised because they knew that those who worked well, those who worked badly, and those who did not work at all would get exactly the same reward—just enough to exist on. So where was the justice, the reward for honest work and the penalty for idleness? The government's solution to the problem was the workhouse. There would be no more outdoor relief. People who needed relief would have to go and live inside the workhouse, where they would find shelter and food, some work and little comfort. It was a harsh remedy, but it succeeded in cutting expenditure, and had the support of tax-payers in county and town alike. Poor people, though, hated and feared the workhouses, which soon had a reputation—not always deserved—for bleak inhumanity. This, some bitterly reflected, was how the Whigs repaid the people who had supported them in the struggle for the great Reform Bill.

Andover Workhouse, from a report in 'Illustrated London News', 1846. There were separate halves for males and females (including exercise yards, dormitories, sick rooms, school rooms for the children) and a common dining hall and chapel. In front were the porter's offices and the Board of Guardians' meeting room. The report says: 'the windows (except at the front) are constructed in such a manner as to deny to the inmates a view of all external objects except a slanting glance at the sky'.

Inside the new Marylebone workhouse, London, 1847.

A school in the East End of London, 1839. It was run on the monitorial system. The master taught the monitors who in turn taught the other pupils. Rewards to be given for good work were hung from the ceiling.

In Britain: pressure from below

The poor would have to help themselves, and they had the power to do it, if only they could think and act together. That was what many people believed, though they did not always agree on the best way to act. One man who had an important plan was Robert Owen (1771-1858). He began his career as an assistant in a clothing store. Through enterprise, intelligence, work and luck he became a successful factory owner in his twenties. He believed that it was possible to form communities where people would live and work freely and happily together, without greed and envy. Between 1814 and 1829 he tried to set an example in his factory at New Lanark, where the workers were well housed, could buy food very cheaply at the factory shop, and had their children well cared for at the factory school. When he went further, and tried to found communities where the members owned everything in common and shared equally the labour and the profits, he failed.

New Lanark. A contemporary print of Owen's self-contained industrial settlement on the Clyde.

The factory school at New Lanark became famous for encouraging each child to learn in his or her own way, and for providing a much greater variety of lessons than most schools. Here the children are giving a display of quadrille dancing.

right: *Interior of the Old Crown Court, Dorchester. Twentieth-century trade unionists restored it to its 1834 appearance in memory of their predecessors who were tried and sentenced here.*

far right: *The 'Martyrs' Tree', Tolpuddle, where the labourers are said to have met to discuss ways of improving their lot. The seat was erected as a memorial in 1934.*

This was probably because he assumed that everyone would be kind, honest and hard-working, and he did not have any effective method of dealing with those who turned out otherwise. But he would not be discouraged. He argued that if the workers themselves jointly owned the factories, farms or mines where they worked, then everybody would be given a fair share of the profits. This was not a new idea. During the early years of the nineteenth century several writers had discussed it, and it had been called *socialism*.

In 1834 Owen launched the Grand National Consolidated Trade Union. The plan was that workers in vast numbers would go on strike, their masters would surrender before this gigantic power, and the workers would peacefully take charge of their industries and run them for everybody's benefit. It sounded easy, and the man proposing it was a rich, successful businessman who ought to know what he was talking about. Within a few weeks the G.N.C.T.U. had half a million members.

It collapsed almost as quickly. Instead of waiting for instructions to act together, local groups began small strikes up and down the country, and failed. Owen's brand of socialism might or might not have worked; it was never tried.

The failure was because great numbers of people proved *not* to be powerful, because they lacked discipline. Also, it is likely that many were scared by the example of what happened to a few who put themselves on the wrong side of the law. Six farm workers of Tolpuddle, Dorset, tried to form a trade union. This was perfectly legal. But they feared the wrath of their employers if they came to hear of the union, so the six made all members swear an oath of secrecy. This was illegal, under a law which was intended to prevent dangerous conspiracies against the state. The local justices of the peace saw the opportunity and grasped it, and the government approved. The six men were sentenced to seven years in the Australian penal settlements. There were widespread protests, agitation in newspapers, a petition to Parliament; but it was two years before the government saw fit to pardon the 'Tolpuddle Martyrs'. The warning was clear.

Though the big scheme had failed so dismally, there were people who thought that co-operation on a small scale would prove more practical and realistic. Why not, for example, get a group of people to band together and buy a shop which would charge the members less for their purchases, or distribute the profits among them? It would be rather like any other company, except that the shareholders who supplied the capital would be people who could afford only tiny amounts. A few early attempts at this sort of thing failed, but in 1844 at Rochdale twenty-eight men each contributed £1 and founded a co-operative shop that prospered. This example encouraged others, until eventually a network of co-operative societies covered Britain. By the end of the century hardly a town was without its 'Co-op'. In this, a movement that had arisen from many small, practical, local enterprises instead of an ambitious nation-wide scheme, the direct self-help of working people ended in triumph, though only after many years.

Not all workers were desperately poor and ignorant. Some

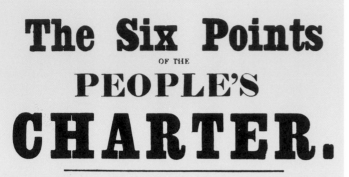

The Six Points
OF THE
PEOPLE'S
CHARTER.

1. A VOTE for every man twenty-one years of age, of sound mind, and not undergoing punishment for crime.

2. THE BALLOT.—To protect the elector in the exercise of his vote.

3. No PROPERTY QUALIFICATION for Members of Parliament —thus enabling the constituencies to return the man of their choice, be he rich or poor.

4. PAYMENT OF MEMBERS, thus enabling an honest trades-man, working man, or other person, to serve a constituency, when taken from his business to attend to the interests of the country.

5. EQUAL CONSTITUENCIES, securing the same amount of representation for the same number of electors, instead of allowing small constituencies to swamp the votes of large ones.

6. ANNUAL PARLIAMENTS, thus presenting the most effectual check to bribery and intimidation, since though a constituency might be bought once in seven years (even with the ballot), no purse could buy a constituency (under a system of universal suffrage) in each ensuing twelvemonth; and since members, when elected for a year only, would not be able to defy and betray their constituents as now.

A contemporary printing of the Charter.

were skilled men, reasonably paid, well read. The members of the London Working Men's Association were of this kind, it seems, and they had never been much impressed by Owen's visions. They believed that solid improvements took time, and there was no miracle cure for poverty; but that it was possible for the working class to make sure that in future laws would be made to look after their interests, instead of for the benefit of landlords and industrialists. They must, in other words, gain control of Parliament. In 1838 one of their leaders, William Lovett, crystallised a lot of discussion into six simple demands which he called the *People's Charter*. Lovett and his friends hoped that it would gradually gain so much support that Parliament would have to admit that it was fair and reasonable. There would be no violence, only argument. The Charter would win by *moral force*.

Lovett had done a fine job. The Charter was brief, clear, and seemed obviously right to thousands of people. Quickly it was adopted by the big Birmingham Political Union, which had already been thinking along similar lines, and thus spread among the workers of the Midlands and the North. Many of these, though, were unskilled, ill paid, unwilling to wait. They planned an enormous petition with millions of signatures, so overwhelming that Parliament would just give in. For behind the petition, unspoken but unmistakable, would be the threat of those millions, the threat of *physical force*.

The leader of the physical force wing of the Chartist movement was an Irish journalist named Feargus O'Connor, a big man with a loud voice, eloquent, quick-witted. He attracted a huge following by his speeches at mass meetings and by his newspaper articles – he founded his own paper, *The Northern Star*. He was, in ancient Greek terms, a demagogue. O'Connor led his followers to think of a general strike, which must quickly bring the government to its knees, or even of armed rebellion. However, he himself was usually careful not to say anything illegal – he left that to people who were more stupid or more honest.

How far were the Chartists prepared to go? Was there a threat of revolution? Did they have the strength and the determination? Certainly they were much better organised than any similar movement previously. Early in 1839 a National Chartist Convention began to sit; some members put M.C. after their names. A huge petition was presented to Parliament, with three million signatures (according to the Chartists; in fact there were 1,200,000). But the House of Commons was not impressed, and in July refused even to debate the petition by 235 votes to 46. The Convention called for a national strike. Nothing happened. In November there was a small, futile attempt at an armed rising in Newport, Monmouthshire, immediately extinguished by soldiers. Lovett, who disapproved both of violence and of bluff and bluster,

The Newport Riot, a contemporary lithograph by J. C. Wilson after W. Howel. The fighting was mainly in and around the Westgate Hotel, where the nine deaths took place and where bullet-holes can still be seen in the porch.

The platform party at a big meeting of the Anti-Corn Law League.

broke with O'Connor. O'Connor tried again, and in 1842 there was a petition which really did have three million signatures. The House of Commons refused to discuss this one by 287 votes to 49. The Chartist leaders had no real idea of what they should do next.

Meanwhile another big popular movement had arisen. In 1839, in Manchester, a league was founded to press for the abolition of the Corn Laws (pages 22 and 36). The appeal was simple: cheap bread. The leaders were, to use an expression which was becoming very important among British people of all classes, *respectable*. John Bright and Richard Cobden were both solid businessmen, earnest speakers but not violent. Abolishing the Corn Laws was only part of what these men wanted. They believed in complete *Free Trade*. They wanted to follow on from Adam Smith and Huskisson, confident that in open competition Britain would thrive. Only weak and inefficient industries needed protection, and the government ought to stop favouring them at the expense of the strong and efficient industries which could do much more to make Britain prosperous.

Such talk of bread and prosperity did not attract the Chartist leaders. They saw the Anti-Corn Law League as a dangerous rival, distracting and dividing the people who might have united behind the People's Charter. One of their speakers explained:

'Not that Corn Law Repeal is wrong: when we get the Charter we will repeal the Corn Laws and all other bad laws. But if you give up your agitation for the Charter to help the Free Traders, they will not help you to get the Charter. Don't be deceived by the middle classes again. You helped them to get their votes – you swelled the cry of "The Bill, the whole Bill and nothing but the Bill". But where are the fine promises they made you? Gone to the winds! They said when they had gotten their votes they would help you to get yours. But they and the rotten Whigs have never remembered you. Municipal Reform has been for their benefit – not for yours. All other reforms the Whigs boast to have effected have been for the benefit of the middle classes – not for yours. And now they want to get the Corn Laws repealed – not for your benefit – but their own. "Cheap Bread!" they cry. But they mean "Low Wages". Do not listen to their cant and humbug. Stick to your Charter. You are veritable slaves without your votes.'

Why was this speaker so bitter against the Whigs, not the

45

Tories? Was it that the Whigs seemed traitors, while the Tories had at least been honest opponents? However, after their great defeat in 1832 the Tories realised – though to many of them it was distasteful – that they would have to attract a lot more popular support. Sir Robert Peel took over the leadership and gave the party a new name: *Conservative*. It meant that their chief purpose was to preserve everything that was good in the traditional British way of life and government. Some young Tories went much further. They had a romantic vision of a past 'Merrie England', when lords were truly noble and kind, and the ordinary people were healthy, hearty and happy, and when both of these great classes respected and liked each other. Now, once again, lords and people should come together against the greedy middle-class businessmen who were causing so much unhappiness with their dirty machines and horrid factory towns. Such notions can easily seem childishly silly, especially when they become mixed up with pseudo-medieval pranks like tournaments, as actually happened at this time. Yet this was not the first nor the last time that many people have felt that the poor gain more from true aristocrats and gentlemen than from those who enrich themselves by buying and selling. Ideals apart, though, there was one hard fact. The Conservative Party remained pledged to protect the landowners and farmers, who still wielded great power in the Lords and in the Commons.

In 1841 the Whigs lost power and Peel became Prime Minister. A series of official reports on conditions in various parts of British industry were being completed and published in the early 1840s, and Peel had to do something about them. These were not exaggerated tales told by political agitators or journalists trying to shock, they were evidence recorded by respectable professional men. Even allowing that normal conditions were not as bad as the most notorious examples, it horrified a great many M.P.s and voters that such things could happen in a country supposed to be free and fair, humane and Christian.

The result was a series of acts passed between 1842 and 1850. Between them, they stopped all females, and males under 10, from working underground in mines; and they reduced the hours that women and children, and eventually men too, could work in textile mills. Thus the 1840s could be thought of as a time when Parliament, controlled as it was by the upper and middle classes, came to accept the duty of protecting the lower classes from the cruellest effects of the Industrial Revolution.

Three extracts from reports on the conditions in different industries laid before Parliament in the early 1840s. Though men were expected to be able to look after themselves, Parliament now felt that it had a duty to protect children and women. The result was, however, that the improvement in conditions affected everybody.

1842 East of Scotland Coal Mines

Fig. 13.

Janet Cumming, eleven years old, bears coals: " I gang with the women at five and come up at five at night; work *all night* on Fridays, and come away at twelve in the day. I carry the large bits of coal from the wall-face to the pit-bottom, and the small pieces called chows in a creel. The weight is usually a hundredweight; does not know how many pounds there are in a hundred-weight, but it is some weight to carry; it takes three journeys to fill a tub of 4 cwt. The distance varies, as the work is not always on the same wall; sometimes 150 fathoms, whiles 250 fathoms. The roof is very low; I have to bend my back and legs, and the water comes frequently up to the calves of my legs. Has no liking for the work; father makes me like it. Never got hurt, but often obliged to scramble out of the pit when bad air was in" (Ibid. No. 1: p. 436, l. 3).

PAINTING ROOM. Temp. 62, air 42.

No. 11.—*Hannah Barker,* aged 40 :—

I am a widow, and managing the children in this room; have been employed in the painting
15 department more than 30 years; have been employed by Messrs. Minton and Boyle 3 years.
I come to work at 7, and leave at 6. I work with other women over-times; always work by
the day, and when we work over time get extra pay: 10s. 6d. per week is our pay, but for
working over time 12s. The children do not work over time; have about 16 girls in this
room, 9 of them are under 13 years of age; all of them are healthy now, but I have buried
20 many out of this room; the smell of the turpentine and paint, and the closeness of the room,
often occasions illness: it has never affected me; I began as early as most. Some of the girls
can write, about 6 of them; all of them can read, all of them attend the Sunday schools.
They are very clean, and moderately well conducted. All of them do not go home to breakfast, the half hour allowed would not enable them to do so, as they live at some distance.
25 Most of them go to dinner. We have holidays, about a month altogether in the year: I think
they live pretty well, and have what is sufficient for children: from my experience I think
that the children who work are better off than those who do not, it must add a little more to
the common stock; the children under my care are better conducted than others in the same
works because I watch over them with the eye of a mother, and teach them their work. In
30 other rooms girls are mixed up indiscriminately with the boys and men, and I think get
bad habits; some are very good, but others you cannot subdue; we are very fortunate in
these works, and seldom have bad characters here. Our masters would not permit it, they
are nice gentlemen, and are very good to them. Mr. Boyle goes round the works every day;
there are not many of such superior characters as they are. I have 6 rooms under my charge,
35 in all containing 70 women and children of all ages; their duties are the same, all paint, and

No. 254.—June 3. *Thomas Parkinson.* At Messrs. Greig's calico-printing-
45 works at Rose Bank, near Edinsfield, Haslingdon Union.

Aged 12 years, 6 months. Works at plaiting pieces of cotton when they pass through the
rollers, this is called tending the drawer, and sometimes works at turning, at the embossing-
machine. This is the hardest work; he has to keep at this from one end of day to t'other,
unless some one turns for him; his uncle gets a boy to turn while he goes home to his meals.
50 Three quarters of an hour is allowed for breakfast, but he comes back in a quarter or 20
minutes. The regular time to come is 6 o'clock morning in summer and 7 in winter; this
morning he came at 4 and does not know what time he shall go away; last Saturday he came
at 4 morning and staid till 10; gets paid for overtime; gets 3s. 6d. a-week; does not know
what he gets for overtime. The place he works in is hot in summer but not too hot in winter.
55 Takes his things off when he is at work and puts them on when he goes out; has not taken
them off to-day. Sometimes he gets his arm burned if he takes his jacket off. Does not
catch cold. Is very tired when he works so late as 10, but it is not so often. Goes to Sun-
day-school; can read and write a bit. Has never worked all night. Works under the
machine-printer, who pays him. Is never beat nor ill-used.

Anti-Corn Law propaganda. This picture was placed inside the crowns of top hats by an enterprising Free Trade hatter.

The 1840s were not a decade of prosperity. Charles Dickens' novels were revealing dramatically conditions and characters at all levels of society, including the lowest. Trade was struggling, and many businessmen, including reformers like Cobden and Bright, feared that the latest Factory Acts would ruin a large part of British industry. If employers had to pay the same wages for shorter hours of work, they argued, they would be forced to put up their prices. Since machines and factories were now spreading in other countries – France, Germany and the U.S.A. especially – these foreigners might be able to sell their goods more cheaply than the British. As it happened, such fears proved wrong. There was an improvement in trade towards the end of the 1840s, and employers found that their workers got through just as much work in the shorter working day because they were less tired.

Yet these years were to be nicknamed 'the Hungry Forties', for harvests were poor and food was not plentiful. Peel accepted many of the arguments of the Free Traders, and began to cut tariffs further. But, though the Anti-Corn Law League kept up its pressure, he remained true to the landowners. Then the unthinkable happened. There was a famine in part of the British Isles, real famine, with thousands of people shrinking into macabre emaciation and dying by the roadside.

Ireland had not been much affected by the Agricultural and Industrial Revolutions. The typical Irishman was a peasant, living in a small cottage or cabin, keeping his family alive on his potato-patch, with a few pigs. It was a desperately poor life – one reason why the British army was full of Irishmen – and there was never much in reserve. In 1845 the potato crop was ruined by a blight. In 1846 it happened again. People were dying in a way Britain had not known since the Black Death. Accurate figures do not exist, but it is estimated that about a million Irish died of starvation during the five years 1846–50, and about another million fled. Emigration continued after the famine; a century later the population of Ireland was little more than half of what it had been in 1845.

Could the British government have saved those people? Many Irish, both in Ireland and across the seas in new lands like the U.S.A., believed that it could. The truth probably is that the government was slow to understand how bad the situation was, that relief was slow in arriving and some of the officials in charge of relief were stupid, callous or corrupt. On the other hand, a great deal of help was sent, and disaster of

above: *An illustration from 'David Copperfield' by Charles Dickens, first published in 1849–50. He tried to shock readers by describing sordid conditions. This is London's waterfront.*

below: *Quite apart from the famine, one of the enduring grievances of the Irish peasants was the ease with which their landlords could turn them out for non-payment of rent. This painting by Lady Butler shows an eviction in 1849. It was painted in 1890 when there was political controversy about the way Ireland should be governed.*

this size was entirely beyond the experience of the people in charge.

Ireland's calamity brought the fall of Robert Peel. He could not bear to think that he might be preventing food from

49

reaching starving people, and in 1846 he repealed the Corn Laws. He was able to do it only because the Whigs, his opponents, voted with him. His own party mostly turned against him as a traitor. Hated and rejected by most Conservatives, Peel had to resign. He died four years later, after a riding accident.

In 1846 the Anti-Corn Law League obtained a victory they had not won, and the Conservative Party split. It turned out that both had been mistaken. Though much more foreign grain was imported, prices did not suffer a sudden collapse, bread did not become cheap, the farmers and landowners were not ruined, the Irish were not saved. In the long run, perhaps the repeal made grain more plentiful and prevented the threat of future shortage, and perhaps it convinced many people that Parliament really did want to be fair and could be persuaded.

That same year the 'railway mania' was at its peak; Parliament passed the record number of 272 acts authorising the construction of lines. Historians may question which would ultimately prove the more important to the people of Britain, the political upheaval or the accelerating pace of the industrial developments.

There were still many who thought that Parliament was not doing enough for the mass of ordinary people, the *working classes*, to use an expression which was becoming common. In 1847 Feargus O'Connor was elected M.P. for Nottingham, and decided to launch one more petition for the People's Charter.

This time the threat of force was much more obvious. O'Connor claimed five million signatures. He planned a vast meeting of Chartists for 10 April 1848. They would assemble, half a million strong, on Kennington Common, and march to Westminster where Feargus O'Connor, their M.P., would present the petition to a suitably chastened Parliament. In February and March revolutions swept across Europe. Capital after capital was the scene of a revolutionary take-over. Could

So far from being ruined, British agriculture was entering what has sometimes been called its 'golden age', from about 1850 to about 1875, when the expanding industrial population demanded more and more food. This cartoon is from a satirical series of articles called 'Mr Pips hys Diary' by Percival Leigh, with illustrations of the 'Manners and Customes of ye Englyshe Drawn from ye Quick' by Richard Doyle. This entry, dated Monday November 19th, 1849, describes the 'Meeting and yearly Dinner of the North Gruntham Agricultural Society at Grumbleton'. The chief speaker, 'Mr. Flummerie', is meant to be Benjamin Disraeli, one of Peel's bitterest critics.

MANNERS AND CVSTOMS OF Yᵉ ENGLYSHE IN 1849. Nᵒ. 38

A BANQVET SHOWINGE Yᵉ FARMERS FRIEND' IMPRESSYNGE ON Yᵉ AGRYCVLTVRAL INTEREST THAT IT IS RVINED.

London be the next? The government wanted to play the whole thing down, and tried to spread the impression that the problem was merely one of directing a particularly big crowd, a job for the police. Soldiers were brought in, but were kept out of sight, while thousands of special constables were enrolled. This coolness paid. The crowd that turned up at Kennington numbered only about 30,000, and seemed as much sight-seers as dedicated Chartists. When they reached Westminster Bridge the police told the leaders that the whole procession must not cross, but that a small group would be allowed to present the petition. It was raining. O'Connor obeyed. The petition was piled into three cabs and rolled away across the bridge. It was the end of Chartism. O'Connor's mind gave way, and he died seven years later, in a lunatic asylum.

When the great petition was examined it was found to contain less than two million signatures, and some of these were flippant forgeries, like 'Mr. Punch'. It added to the atmosphere of silly anticlimax, and there were many who were glad to think that Chartism had all been a big sham. But it was not a sham. There had been hundreds of thousands of perfectly genuine signatures, and the movement had been strong enough to survive two humiliating failures. The six points were not dead; most of them became law within the next two or three generations, so it could be said that Chartist ideals were victorious in the end, though the movement itself was beaten.

Chartism leaves historians with some important questions to which there are no easy, certain answers. Why did Britain, which seemed to be suffering so much more strain and discontent than other European countries as a result of the industrial changes, avoid revolution? During the 1832 crisis Wellington said that the British people were 'quiet'. Was this the answer – that they were naturally unwilling to have violence in politics? Or had the reforms of the 1830s and 1840s been enough to make most of them think that Parliament could be influenced and that this was more likely to produce solid improvements than any revolutionary upheaval? Perhaps the industrial developments were bringing opportunities as well as difficulties, and many of the most enterprising workers were seizing upon these instead of revolutionary schemes. Perhaps, even, movements like the G.N.C.T.U. and Chartism were partly responsible for Parliament's beginning to see that it must do something to protect the working classes. When Parliament accepted this duty, perhaps the Chartists gained their main objective and at the same time saved Britain from revolution.

3 The year of revolutions

France

Once again a series of revolutions exploded across Europe, and the people of Paris set them off.

Why, only eighteen years after 1830, did the Parisians want yet another revolution? One reason may have been that many of them, as we saw, had felt cheated by the result of 1830; instead of the republic they thought they had won, they got a king who personified the rich middle class, the *bourgeoisie*. Though nothing like Britain – the French were to remain a nation of farmers and peasants for several generations yet – France was beginning to feel the Industrial Revolution. Since 1830 the number of steam engines in France had increased more than eight-fold. In the mining villages of the north-east and the textile factories of Lyons people were undergoing the hardships that caused discontent in Britain. When trade was bad, as it was in 1846–7, men lost their jobs and poverty bit even harder. King Louis Philippe's successive governments were able to quell the occasional outbursts of violence in big towns, but not one of them seemed to have ideas about how to tackle the problems of poverty.

Other Frenchmen, however, had cures – at least on paper.

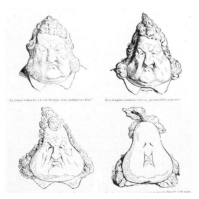

The cartoonist Philipon transformed Louis Philippe into a pear; the French word *poire* also means, colloquially, a dullard, one who is easily deceived.

Socialism was one, but a different type from Robert Owen's in Britain. His had been *guild socialism*, so called because it meant associations or guilds of workers running their own crafts, trades or industries. This other form was *state socialism*; here the government of the state would own everything, would be the only employer and would, of course, treat everyone justly. And what was just treatment? Louis Blanc was the best-known socialist writer of the time, and he gave a definition that became famous: 'To each according to his needs, from each according to his ability.' Some thought this noble, others naïve. Blanc also asserted that every man had a right to work, and that if he could not find a job the government ought to employ and pay him. Starry-eyed or not, these ideals appealed to many people who found little to admire in the hard-headed business-like attitude of the bourgeois monarchy.

That monarchy was dull, too. Despite his attempt to collect some cheap glory by carrying on with the conquest of Algeria (where the newly formed Foreign Legion saved French lives by doing much of the dirty work) there was no touch of glamour, or even dignity, about the citizen king. A generation had grown up since 1815 who had not known what Napoleonic glory had cost in blood and toil. They even found an epic, heroic quality in the disasters of 1812–15. Bonapartism grew. Bonapartists believed that their hero had not only been a mighty leader in war, but a wise lawgiver and administrator whose only desire had been to protect and enrich the French people. Napoleon's son had died young, but he had a nephew called Louis Napoleon. This man thought that there were so many Bonapartists in France that he could lead a successful rising. He was badly mistaken and was imprisoned in a fortress, from which he eventually escaped to England. (He enrolled as a special constable against the Chartist threat in April 1848.) All the same, King Louis Philippe tried to filch some popularity from the Bonapartist fashion; in 1840 he had Napoleon's body brought back from St Helena and buried splendidly in Paris.

But the bourgeois monarchy was not exciting. It was said: 'La France s'ennuie' – 'France is getting bored.'

The revolution was not planned. It happened almost accidentally in February 1848. A big meeting was organised in Paris where there would be speeches demanding reforms. The government banned it. There were angry protests, and barricades went up in some streets. The National Guard came out – and sided with the rebels. Then the king fled to England. It had been even more sudden than in 1830. Nobody had any plans ready, but a couple of Paris newspapers printed lists of men who, in their opinion, ought to form a provisional government. These men simply took over.

That was how a mixed group of idealistic talkers and writers found themselves in charge of France. Most of them agreed on one thing, Liberty. By this they understood free elections, with every man entitled to vote; freedom of speech; freedom of the press; freedom of religion; and a republican form of government. It was easy enough to order all that. Much more difficult was the problem of how to satisfy the poor and the unemployed.

Few members of the new government believed that Louis Blanc's theories would work. On the other hand, his ideas were very popular in the narrow, squalid streets of the poorer quarters of Paris. Besides, nobody else seemed to have any ideas at all. So Blanc was authorised to set up National Workshops in Paris. Here work was guaranteed for anyone who applied. Workless men flocked in, at first from Paris, soon from many parts of France. Presently there was no work left. Senseless jobs were invented, like digging holes and filling them in again. Even this could not keep everybody busy, and sometimes for days on end men were paid for coming and doing nothing. The scheme became an extravagant farce. People mocked. Blanc complained that it was not being run the way he had intended, and that his enemies were deliberately causing mistakes. His critics said that these were just hollow excuses and that the scheme had been wrong-headed from the start, bound to attract lazy ruffians to live at the expense of hardworking taxpayers. As disagreements became more open, thousands of Parisians demonstrated in the streets in favour of Blanc and socialism. But Paris was not France.

In late April elections were held for an Assembly which would draw up a new constitution for France, and only about a tenth of the members elected were socialist. But when the Assembly met, in Paris, a crowd gathered and tried to force it to appoint a socialist government. The National Guard was called out, and this time it did not sympathise with the rebels, so the Assembly was saved. After this fright, the Assembly decided that the National Workshops were the centre of trouble; they were said to be supporting 100,000 men and to be a perfect recruiting-ground for violent mobs. Therefore in June the Assembly ordered them to close down. In the poor quarters of Paris this meant that far less money would be coming in. Up went the barricades once more. But this time it was not to be

A sketch commenting on the efficiency of the National Workshops published in the Paris 'Journal pour Rire'.

below: *Street fighting in the Rue St Antoine, June 1848. A contemporary lithograph.*

the bloodless expulsion of a weary old king. The Assembly sent in the army. The rebels were well armed, and the troops lost 9,000 dead, but after four savage days, 23–6 June, they crushed the rising. 'The June Days' left bitter memories on both sides. The Assembly would make sure that there was no socialism in the new republic.

By November the Assembly had drafted the constitution of the Second French Republic. After the disorders, it is not surprising that it gave plenty of power to the President, so that he could enforce law and order. In December the election was held for President. The likeliest candidate seemed to be the general who had smashed the barricades in June, but when the

Louis Napoleon, shown above in a photograph, appealed openly to the legend of military glory left by his uncle, Napoleon Bonaparte. The upper print pictures the distribution of eagle standards— symbols of imperial power—to the regiments of the French army in May 1852. The lower print is an almost comically naive view of Louis Napoleon's entry into Paris the following October.

votes were counted he had only one-and-a-half million votes. The winner, with five million votes, was Louis Napoleon Bonaparte.

Was history repeating itself? Yet there were huge differences between 1848 and 1799. The new Bonaparte was not a victorious general grasping power in a moment of danger. This time the danger was over, and the victorious general was voted down. The new Napoleon was a civilian and was elected legally. Perhaps one reason for his success was that he had not been involved in the troubles earlier in the year.

For a while Louis Napoleon was content to be a president. He knew that even if the Parisians were inclined towards revolutionary ideas, most of the French were not. Many of them, in fact, would still have preferred the old way, a steady government guided firmly by Church and king. In France, revolutionaries had usually been against the Church, had accused it of misusing its wealth and power and had tried to take the wealth and power themselves. But religion was still very important to millions of devout French Catholics, and Louis Napoleon determined to earn their support. When the Pope had trouble with revolutionaries in Rome, a French army was sent to his aid. At home, the President·gave permission for church schools in some places to take over from state schools. (At the same time he tightened the government's powers over state schools, for he was not going to let any party gain power at his expense; and every ruler understands the importance of what children are taught to believe.) Seeing what the President was doing, the revolutionaries were furious, and in their anger they played into his hands. They spoke and wrote so violently that it was easy for Louis Napoleon to suggest that only his great power kept these wild men from armed revolt.

Gradually Louis Napoleon appointed his supporters as ministers until he could be quite sure of his government. He got rid of civil servants who seemed likely to try to obstruct his orders. His agents quietly supervised public meetings and newspapers. He altered the election laws so that only men who had dwelt in the same place for at least three years could vote; this rule excluded workers who changed jobs and towns frequently – just the people, it was thought, who would be likely to vote for revolutionary parties.

After two years of this sort of preparation, Louis Napoleon began to plan his own re-election. According to the constitution of 1848 a president's term lasted four years and he could not be re-elected immediately. Louis Napoleon did not want to rush things, and as early as the summer of 1851 he tried to get the constitution altered so as to allow him a second term. He got a majority of the Assembly to agree, but not quite a big enough majority to allow him legally to change the constitution. He had miscalculated. Now he would have to copy his uncle, and use force. One morning a few months later Paris awoke to find troops in position everywhere. Opponents of the President were arrested. Louis Napoleon had given the order, and the army had obeyed. The date had been chosen carefully. It was 2 December, the day of Austerlitz.

Louis Napoleon proclaimed that he had taken control because he believed that the French people wanted him to, because they were tired of the wranglings of politicians in the Assembly. He was proved right. A few riots, mostly in Paris, were soon extinguished by the troops. A plebiscite held on 21 December supported him by the sort of majority his uncle used to get: $7\frac{1}{2}$ million votes to 640,000. Now he felt confident in proclaiming a new constitution, which gave the President almost complete power.

Within a few months his devoted Senate and Assembly requested him to assume the title of emperor. Bowing to the wishes of his people, of course, he made himself emperor on 2 December 1852.

He did not call himself Napoleon II, but III. True Bonapartists reckoned that Napoleon I's son had been Napoleon II. The new form of government, however, was called the Second Empire. Thus the Second Republic was buried four years after the revolution of 1848, and in fact it had already been dead for some time.

Louis Napoleon had given a textbook example of how a fairly popular and unscrupulous political leader could gain a supreme position, all in the name of the people. He used every trick. He appealed to religion, he played on the fear of disorder, he twisted the rules, he bribed and bullied and finally used armed force. But the French people did support him.

So we are left with the question: was there really a French Revolution in 1848? Or was it only a Parisian outburst that the government of Louis Philippe failed to meet firmly or sensibly? If economic hardship, widespread discontent and massive demands for improvements are causes of revolution, then Britain seems to have been a more likely country than France, but things did not work out like that

The Habsburg Empire

If Paris inspired revolutions, Vienna was the capital of reaction.

The people of Austria itself were German. For nearly four centuries their rulers, the Habsburg family, had been regularly elected Holy Roman Emperors. When in 1806 the old Empire was at last scrapped, the Habsburg title was changed to Emperor of Austria. But when, in 1815, the new Germanic Confederation was formed, naturally the Austrian Emperor was recognised as the senior member, and his representative presided over the meetings of its Diet. Metternich took full advantage of this. He encouraged the other members of the Confederation to keep their liberal subjects firmly under control, to censor the press, and not to allow any power to elected assemblies. Metternich was detested by liberals everywhere, but he remained the power behind the emperor for more than thirty years.

Only a few of the many provinces of the Austrian Empire, though, were German. Many other nations or parts of nations had been collected by the Habsburgs over the centuries, and most of these could look back proudly to the days of their own independence and greatness. The Czechs of Bohemia, the

LANGUAGES
Slavonic
  Polish
  Czech
  Slovak
  Little Russian (Ruthenian)
  White Russian
  Serbo–Croat
  Bulgarian
Latin
  French
  Italian
  Romanian
Teutonic
  High German
  Low German
Finno-Ugrian
  Magyar

Apart from a few regions traditionally linked to the old Holy Roman Empire, only the German-speaking parts had membership of the Germanic Confederation

Nationalities within the Habsburg Empire 1848
— Germanic Confederation
— Habsburg Empire
0   100 miles
0   150 km

In most parts of Europe countryfolk still wore national costume, and sometimes this influenced characteristic national military uniforms. These pictures of costumes and uniforms of four parts of the Habsburg Empire (from left to right, Bohemia, Austria, Hungary, Tyrol) are from a French book of costumes of the world, published in 1870.

Magyars of Hungary, the Italians of Milan and Venice – all had played leading roles in the development of Europe, and they were not alone. Serbs and Croats, Poles and Romanians had their own languages, cultures and traditions of past glory. These peoples owed obedience only to the Austrian Emperor because he happened to be, for example, King of Bohemia, or Hungary, also. They were not Austrians, and many of them resented the way German-speakers seemed to rule the whole empire. When a liberal from one of these nations talked about freedom, he naturally meant freedom for his own people.

As yet the Industrial Revolution had hardly touched the Habsburg Empire. Nevertheless, there were many great cities, some of them the old capitals of kingdoms. Crowds could gather, newspapers and gossip could circulate – the coffee-house was a Viennese invention – and there were a great many people in these cities who supported liberal ideas. Many were impatient by 1848. The news from Paris touched them off. The sister cities of Buda and Pest were first to rise, on 3 March. Hungarian liberals crowded into the streets and took control. There was no bloodshed. After all the talk that had gone on for years, it seemed natural. The most prominent leader was a politician and journalist named Louis Kossuth, a flamboyant

orator with a passionate belief in the importance of the Magyars and of himself, and a gift for convincing masses of people that he was right. He and his colleagues now demanded that the Kingdom of Hungary should have a parliament with full powers to appoint a government, quite separate from Austria which ought to have its own parliament.

Vienna caught the revolutionary feeling. Here there was a little fighting in the streets, but the government gave in on 13 March, and Metternich fled. The emperor agreed to a liberal government in Buda-Pest, for Hungary, and another in Vienna, for the rest of the empire. In both capitals these governments set to work on reforms. Because most of the people of the empire, whatever their nationality, were peasants, the most important reforms were those which abolished the feudal privileges and restrictions that still existed, and made it easier for peasants to own land.

Meanwhile Bohemia and other parts of the empire were claiming their own parliaments or assemblies, their own con-stitutions. The only place where there was serious fighting was Italy. There was a rising in Milan, and the imperial troops were driven out. The Milanese appealed for help to their neighbours, the Piedmontese. Liberals in the government of Sardinia–

Piedmont persuaded their king that this was an opportunity, and so he declared war against Austria. While this was going on, Venice declared herself once more a free republic.

Beyond the Habsburg frontiers, all across the Germanic Confederation, the same sort of thing was happening. Seemingly paralysed by the Habsburg collapse, kings and princes everywhere were granting constitutions and inviting liberals to form governments. As the spring of 1848 turned to summer, it looked as though the spirit of liberal revolution had effortlessly seized almost all Europe.

Within a year it was all over, and the European revolution had perished. And once again it was what happened in the Habsburg Empire that decided what happened elsewhere.

Many a revolution has begun gently and then been taken over by extremists. In May 1848 it looked as though this was happening in Austria. The emperor fled from Vienna and a Committee of Public Safety took power. Meanwhile in Prague Czech nationalists summoned a congress which was intended to bring together representatives of all the Slav nations; this was bound to mean hostility to Germans. Excited crowds filled the streets again, and during the confusion somebody shot the wife of the general commanding the imperial troops stationed there. The general was already worried and angry; this was the final provocation. He brought up more troops and on 17 June his guns opened fire on the city. The people of Prague were aghast at this, their revolutionary enthusiasm faded, and the imperial army took a firm grip on Bohemia. This was the first turning-point.

Next month came the turning-point in Italy. The Austrian general, eighty-two-year-old Radetzky, had seemed to be losing, and the emperor ordered him to make a truce. Radetzky refused, fought the Piedmontese army and defeated it at Custozza on 24 July, and next month marched back into Milan.

The third, and probably the most important, turn was of a different kind. The others had occurred when imperial generals had struck back at the revolutionaries, but this one was a case of revolutionaries turning against one another. As we saw, the Hungarian revolutionaries claimed to govern the Kingdom of Hungary. But within the borders of the old kingdom there dwelt not only Magyars, but people of many other nations. Were they also to be free? Kossuth and his friends had no intention of giving up what they saw as the ancient rights of Hungary; to others it seemed that the Magyars were refusing

left: *Joseph Radetzky, Count of Radetz; born in 1766, he joined the army in 1785 and rose to high command in the Napoleonic wars. This portrait shows old 'Father Radetzky', the idol of the army, about the time of his greatest triumphs. The march written in his honour by the elder Johann Strauss, 1804–49, became almost a second Austrian national anthem. Radetzky died in 1858.*

below: *Kossuth, 1802–94, shown as a heroic figure in a popular Hungarian print of the time. The inscription means: 'Long live Louis Kossuth!'.*

ÉLJEN KOSSUTH LAJOS.

to their own subjects the liberty they claimed for themselves from the Austrians. In fact, the governor of Croatia thought, there was more to be gained from the emperor than from the Hungarians, so he led the Croats to attack Hungary in September. As fighting spread, Serbs and Romanians also rose and began guerrilla operations against the Hungarians.

Now the reaction against the revolutionaries grew stronger and more violent. Imperial troops, led by the victor of Prague, marched on Vienna, bombarded the city, and took it on 31 October. Several revolutionary leaders were executed. Then the army moved into Hungary. Beset by many foes, the Magyars fought with skill and daring. For a while it looked as though they might redeem by their valour what they had lost by stupid selfishness. They thrust the imperial army out of Hungary in April 1849 and declared the country a republic, with Kossuth president. But this only increased their enemies. The Tsar had no desire to see a revolutionary republic so near to his own empire, and he offered to help in crushing it. The Austrian emperor accepted. Between the Austrian and Russian armies the Hungarian revolutionaries were soon overwhelmed. Then the local Austrian general set about teaching the rebels a lesson, using bullet, rope and whip with a determination that made him detested not only in Hungary, but among newspaper-readers all over Europe. Kossuth himself fled, loudly blaming others for the disasters his own arrogance had done

most to bring about; he was received as a hero when he visited Britain and the United States.

So the 'patchwork quilt' of the Habsburg Empire was restored. The forces that nearly tore it apart were partly nationalist, partly liberal. But the army remained loyal, and that was what decided the issue. The centre of Europe would go on as before.

A few traces of the 1848 revolution did survive. The peasants kept the liberties they had gained. Above all, 1848 could not be forgotten. It was both warning and encouragement to both government and liberals; neither side really wanted another year like that. In December 1848 the emperor abdicated, so that a fresh, more hopeful look could be given to the battered monarchy. The new emperor was a youth of eighteen, Francis Joseph, and he was still Austrian Emperor when he died in 1916.

Germany

No people had been more influenced by Romanticism than the Germans, and none had shown more nationalist enthusiasm during the War of Liberation against Napoleon, in 1813. But the Congress of Vienna did little to satisfy such feelings. The Germanic Confederation that it set up was loose and weak. It had a Diet which met at Frankfurt, but this consisted only of

representatives of the kings and princes of the different member states; naturally these people were not going to create a strong government which could limit their own freedom and power. Equally, they were not going to give up any of their powers to liberals.

Among the many small German states there were two giants. We have already looked at the first, Austria. The other, Prussia, had been Austria's rival since the days of Frederick the Great and Maria Theresa. In the War of Liberation Prussia had seemed a shining example to all Germans. Her leaders had freed the peasants from serfdom and compulsory labour. They had expanded and improved schools and colleges. They had transformed the army – no more of the old machine-like discipline enforced by beatings, but a big force of short-service conscripts and volunteers who may have lacked the skill of the former professionals but who had zeal and dash. After the war, however, Prussia deflated. There were no more reforms. From time to time elected assemblies were tried, but the king would not allow any of them any real power; Prussia, the king and his advisers were determined, would remain a genuine monarchy, not some sort of constitutional parliamentary mixture. Austria was senior member of the Diet, and Prussia resented it. The Prussian government wanted to take the lead in some

way, and found its opportunity in trade. All those frontiers within the Germanic Confederation, each with its customs barriers, hindered trade. The situation was most awkward for a sprawling state, as Prussia now was. In 1819 Prussia signed an agreement with one of her small neighbours that both would charge the same customs and that there should be no barriers to trade between them. This customs union, or *Zollverein*, seemed a good idea to other states, who gradually joined. As the Prussian Zollverein grew, some outsiders began to fear a Prussian take-over of all German trade, so they tried to form rival customs unions of their own. But by this time it was too late, for the Prussian Zollverein was strong enough not only to help its members by lowering customs but to damage its rivals by raising customs against their goods. So eventually most German states decided that they would be more prosperous with Prussia than against her, and by 1848 most were in the Zollverein.

Metternich was too slow in realising how Prussia was increasing her influence in this way, but in other respects Austria remained the leader of the Confederation. This was one of the reasons why liberals were kept down, throughout Germany. In 1830 a few German princes granted powers to their assemblies and became constitutional rulers within their states, but the Diet reacted in 1832 by declaring that there must be no more of these changes. Next year some would-be revolutionaries made an attempt to seize Frankfurt, so the Diet set up a committee which organised and combined the anti-revolutionary work of all the different police forces. In this way there was unity throughout Germany, but it was a union of princes; not at all the unity that liberals wanted.

The news of the 1848 revolution in Paris, and then the astounding collapse of Habsburg authority in Buda-Pest and Vienna, excited liberals in all the German states and shook the confidence of the princes. But one of the two giants remained, Prussia. What sort of an example would the Prussian government set? In Berlin liberals built barricades in the streets. The army attacked them, but the king immediately ordered his troops to stop. King Frederick William IV was confused. He sympathised with much of what the liberals wanted, but he

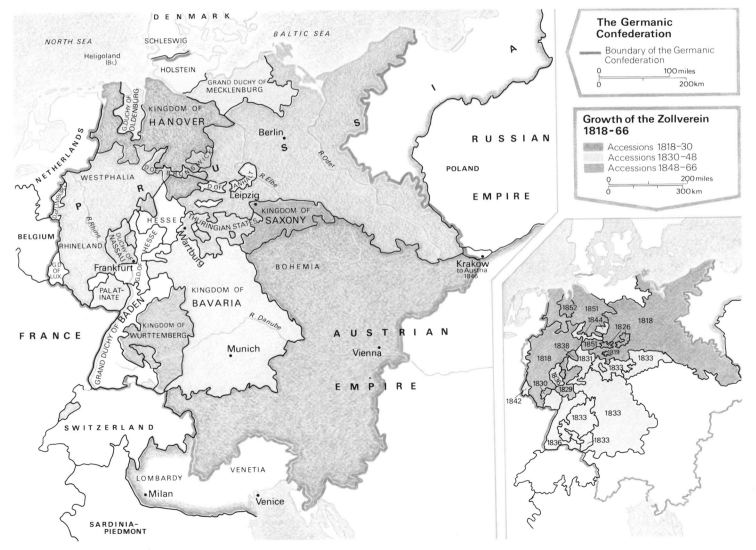

also believed that kings were appointed by God and therefore could not hand over their responsibility and power to anyone else. Now, rather than permit bloodshed, he promised to grant a constitution and summon an assembly. In state after state the other German rulers did the same. As in France and Austria, it seemed that the old regime had lost its energy, and crumbled.

Already at the beginning of March liberals from many states had taken the initiative. They met and called for a 'preliminary parliament' with members from all parts of Germany. This met before the month was out, and in turn arranged that there should be elections for an assembly representing the whole of Germany, every man being entitled to vote. This new body was speedily assembled, on 18 May, and is known as the Frankfurt Parliament. It was probably the best-educated parliament in history; about one eighth

were professors, one quarter lawyers. The speeches were intelligent, earnest – and lengthy.

This outstandingly gifted and well-meaning assembly was a dismal failure. Why? The answer is brutally simple: it lacked force. The Frankfurt Parliament had no troops and no money except what the various German states contributed. At first the rulers of the states went along with the liberal tide, but gradually the princes and their old advisers saw that as long as their officials and, most important, their soldiers continued to obey them, they still held the real power. The liberals had to rely on persuading; life would be so much better, they said, if people would do as they told them. But meanwhile they were not working any miracles.

With things in this undecided state, it was bad luck for the Frankfurt Parliament that it was challenged by a foreign

Meeting of the preliminary parliament at Frankfurt, as shown in the Leipzig 'Illustrierte Zeitung' of 20 May 1848. It is being held in St Paul's Church, and above the gallery are draped the national colours, black, red and gold, as used in the War of Liberation.

country. The King of Denmark claimed the two duchies of Schleswig and Holstein, where the people were partly Danish and partly German, The whole affair was very complicated, especially when other countries became involved; a few years later a British prime minister despairingly joked that only three people had ever understood it properly, and of these three one was dead, one had gone mad, and the third – himself – had forgotten. But to most Germans it looked simple enough: Germans in the duchies were being forced to become Danes. This had to be stopped. What was the Frankfurt Parliament going to do about it?

Without troops, what *could* the Parliament do? It had to ask for help, and Prussia was the obvious state to supply troops. The Prussian government, unwillingly doing the bidding of the Parliament, sent a force to Schleswig-Holstein. There followed skirmishes, truces, talks and eventually a compromise settlement. But long before this it had become obvious that the Frankfurt Parliament could do nothing on its own. Many Germans, possibly most, had believed that national unity would mean strength and dignity. Instead, even puny Denmark could disregard the German national parliament. It was humiliating. Nobody respected weakness.

During late 1848 and early 1849, while the parliament debated its wordy way towards a new constitution to replace the Confederation, the kings and princes were regaining more confidence. In Prussia the king appointed fresh advisers who were not liberals and who believed that the government should govern firmly. They encouraged him to dissolve the liberal Prussian assembly that he had permitted after the Berlin rising. He did so and, as his army was loyal, there was no trouble. Once again in Prussia the king was sole master. Meanwhile the Austrian revolution was over, and the emperor's government was determined to reassert itself in Germany as well as within its own frontiers. Previously, as we saw on page 56, only the German-speaking parts of the Habsburg Empire had been members of the Germanic Confederation. Now the Austrian government insisted that the whole empire must be regarded as a single, undivided country, and that all of it must have membership of the Confederation. But could a German national parliament possibly admit all those other nations (especially Slav nations) as if they were Germans, and let Austria dictate what the new Germany should be? At Frankfurt they said no. They thought it better to reject Austria altogether, to end the long centuries of Habsburg leadership. Instead they turned to the King of Prussia, and offered him the title of Emperor of the Germans.

So it fell to King Frederick William to decide the result of the 1848 revolution in Germany. If he accepted, he would be raising his House of Hohenzollern to the highest possible rank, and winning a great triumph over the Habsburgs. But what sort of emperor would he be? What authority would he have, what power? He would have to accept the new constitution of Germany: a parliament elected by all adult male Germans would control the laws, the money, the ministers. Could a king who believed in his Divine Right to rule agree to follow the counsels of anyone except God? Besides, Frederick William knew that several of the other German kings and princes did not want him to accept the title. For weeks he hesitated. Two of his remarks became famous:

> 'Frederick the Great would have been the man for you; I am no great ruler.'

and

> 'I cannot pick up a crown from the gutter.'

At last, from timidity or from pride, he refused.

The Frankfurt Parliament's attempt to create a united German Empire with a liberal constitution had failed. The governments of the German states, now back under the control of their kings and princes, ordered their representatives to come home from Frankfurt, and soon afterwards those members who refused to leave the parliament were ejected by soldiers.

All that remained to be settled was whether the Germanic Confederation would be restored exactly as before. Austria said yes, Prussia tried to claim the lead for herself; but when it came to a confrontation and war seemed inevitable, Prussia backed down. After this 'humiliation', as many Prussians bitterly called it, the old Confederation went on as before, with the Austrian representative presiding over the Diet.

Of all the revolutions of 1848, that in Germany was probably the most truly liberal and national. It represented every part of a great country, it was not inspired by hatred of any foreign power, its leaders were moderate and reasonable. But they were compelled to rely on Prussia, and Prussia was a broken reed.

Italy

We saw on page 58 what happened in 1848 in northern Italy. By autumn the Sardinian–Piedmontese government was glad to sign a truce with the Austrians.

In southern Italy, too, the year ended in a sort of balance. The Kingdom of the Two Sicilies had, like so many other places in that year, seen a quick, easy liberal take-over. But in May the king's loyal regiments, largely Swiss mercenaries, restored

Italy 1848

him to power in Naples. However, the other half of the kingdom, Sicily, still had to be brought to order.

With the rival forces containing each other in the north and the south, the centre of Italy could get on with its own revolution, if it chose, without a great deal of intervention from either direction.

Before going on to the story of the revolution in Rome, it would be useful to ask why there were these outbreaks in the different parts of Italy.

In the south the answer may seem obvious. Naples was poverty-stricken. The villages were wretched and the slums of the city itself were the most notoriously foul in all Europe. But what seems obvious is not always true, and poverty need not cause revolution. The poor peasants and the *lazzaroni* of the slums were often fanatically loyal to their Church and their king. Some secret societies which claimed to protect the poor and oppressed became in fact gangs of murderous thieves, like the Sicilian Mafia, and the bandits who lurked in the mountains of Calabria were not quite the picturesque Robin Hoods that some romantics imagined them to be. Still, there was so much wrong that there were always people ready to plot and revolt. Indeed, the rising in Sicily and then Naples was probably the only one of the 1848 revolutions that owed nothing to the example of Paris; it happened a month before the Paris rising.

In northern Italy, by contrast, the risings could hardly have been caused by bad government; by Italian standards the Austrian administration there was efficient and just. It was hated, though – because it was foreign. Nationalism more than liberalism inspired the plots and risings. And when plotters and rebels were caught and punished they became martyrs, and the Austrians were reviled as cruel tyrants.

The middle of Italy was mainly the Papal States, with a government as reactionary as anywhere else. But in 1846 a new Pope was elected, Pius IX, who sympathised with many liberal ideas. He began to reform the government of the Papal States, gradually moving towards constitutional government. He set up councils to advise his ministers, relaxed the censorship of the press and freed political prisoners. Ever since the time of Voltaire many Europeans had taken it for granted that the Church was always against anything enlightened or liberal. This reforming Pope not only shocked reactionaries who had come to depend on the Church, he also upset liberals who had enjoyed attacking the Church; but the main effect probably

Italian national dress, from the same source as the illustration on page 57. There are regional variations among the women's costumes. The uniforms are very similar to Sardinian-Piedmontese uniforms of 1848–9.

was to encourage movements towards reform and revolution throughout Italy.

During 1848 Pius IX changed his mind. Roman liberals, excited by the news from abroad and encouraged by the reforms already made, demanded more. Pius appointed a new prime minister, a moderate liberal, but this did not satisfy the demands. The prime minister was murdered and there was a rising in the city, and the Pope was forced to appoint a strongly liberal government. He took the first opportunity to escape from Rome and seek the protection of the King of Naples. So in February 1849 the liberals proclaimed a republic in Rome and invited Mazzini to lead it.

By now, though, big powers were becoming concerned. Austria was a Catholic monarchy and was responsible for ruling part of Italy near the Papal States. France had no Italian territory but, as we saw on page 55, contained millions of Catholics whom the president wanted to please. So the rulers of both Austria and France thought it advisable to help the Pope, and neither wanted the other to get in first. Austria, however, was still busy with Hungary, and Sardinia–Piedmont ended the truce and resumed the war in northern Italy. Then, on 23 March 1849, old Radetzky defeated the Piedmontese so

Pius IX; born Giovanni Maria Mastai-Ferretti 1792, Pope 1846, died 1878.

thoroughly at Novara that it was obvious that the war would soon be over and the Austrian army free to intervene in Rome. This was enough to make France act. In April a French army landed on the coast about fifty miles from Rome.

65

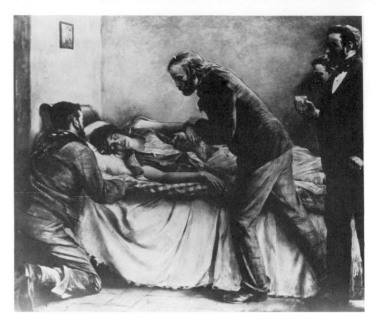

In later years, after his successes, Garibaldi became the subject of romantic pictures of differing degrees of skill. Here are two such. One shows him charging the French. The other shows him, with his eldest son, at the bedside of his dying wife.

The Roman republicans refused to believe it. France, home of revolution and republicanism, could not seriously mean to attack a sister republic; it must just be a diplomatic gesture. But they were mistaken. The French commanders thought that a sudden attack would bring them a quick, cheap victory. And they too were mistaken. The French were hurled back by a scratch force of Italians led by a man who was to be one of the romantic legends of the nineteenth century – Giuseppe Garibaldi.

Garibaldi's life so far had been an adventure story. A sailor, then a revolutionary, he had had to flee to South America. In Uruguay's struggle for independence against her bigger neighbours he won fame and victory as privateer, naval commodore and finally as general of the Italian Legion. So he was already a skilled commander on sea and land when in 1848 he sailed back to fight for Italy's freedom. During the war in the north he and his volunteers became famous for their daring exploits against Austrian detachments. These were the men who now led the defence of Rome against the French.

After the repulse of the first attack there was a pause. Negotiations began for peace. The French received reinforcements and again they attacked suddenly. Again Garibaldi threw them back, and for a month his men held Rome against

the French army. But the struggle was hopeless, and at last even he had to admit it. He handed the city over to the French and marched away.

Venice was still holding out against the Austrians, and Garibaldi's force tried to go there. But Austrian troops closed in on them. Garibaldi struggled on until only a few of his men remained, hiding in the pine woods near Ravenna. Here his wife, exhausted by hardship and illness, died. Now at last he gave up, and fled from Italy. In August Venice surrendered.

All Italy was back under its old governments. The only noticeable change was that a French garrison remained in Rome to protect the Pope.

Had the Italian uprisings achieved anything or proved anything? This was the first time all parts of Italy had risen, but had they risen together? Or for the same cause? This time, too, a king had joined. But was it because he was a liberal, or a nationalist, or because he thought he saw a chance of gaining lands from Austria? Motives were confused. But one thing had become perfectly clear. Austria would have proved quite strong enough to put down the risings even if France, for Louis Napoleon's own reasons, had not given the death-blow to the 1848 revolutions in Italy.

In the name of the People

The first half of the century closed with the old regime seemingly victorious everywhere. Yet there was a vast difference between this time and the eighteenth century. Then Europe had been the stage for war after war, between firmly established monarchs (most of them despots) employing professional armies. Now Europe had been free from wars between major states since 1815. It was the longest period of international peace since modern international politics had begun, nearly four centuries before. But Europe had not been quiet. The continual revolutions, failing but persisting, were just as remarkable as the absence of wars.

These revolutions had spread very wide. We have seen how they covered most of Europe in 1848, but even this does not give the full picture. Spain and Portugal had risen in 1820, but were not mentioned in 1830 or 1848. The reason is not that they were now placid, but that both were continually in strife over their own problems. In each country the quarrel was over who should succeed to the throne – an ancient enough cause of civil wars. But this time there was a resemblance to the revolutionary–reactionary struggle that seemed to be involving all Europe, for in both Spain and Portugal the reigning monarchs and their governments were constitutional while the rebel claimants stood for old-fashioned monarchy, 'by the grace of God' and not by permission of any parliament. The Spanish Carlists and Portuguese Miguelists were not only fighting because they thought Don Carlos and Dom Miguel were rightful kings, but because they preferred the old ways to liberalism.

There had been many revolts in Europe during the years between 1815 and 1848, and each had its own reasons. Sometimes the rebels demanded what they understood as liberty – votes for all men, for example, and freedom of the press. Others were more eager to unite a divided nation or expel a foreign ruler. But most had this in common: they were ready to sacrifice themselves and others for a cause which was not devotion to a religion, or loyalty to a royal house, or even lust for wealth. Their cause was to benefit the great mass of men, women and children who made up the nation. They fought not in the name of God or the King, but in the name of the People.

In Spain both sides claimed to be fighting for the people's rights but both sides had to seize food from the people This drawing shows Carlist cavalry, recognizable by their large berets – often red with yellow tassel – requisitioning cattle in Aragon.

4 Mid century

'The workshop of the world'

Among the refugees of all shades of opinion who found safe lodging in Britain when defeated in their own countries, there was a German journalist called Karl Marx, Jewish by descent but not by religion. In 1848 he and Friedrich Engels had issued *The Communist Manifesto*, expounding their own sort of socialism and calling for the working classes of all nations to join in wresting power from the ruling classes. 'Workers of the world, unite!' was their slogan. Engels, a businessman, had already spent some time in Britain and had studied the harsh conditions in which many industrial workers lived. Marx settled in London and spent the rest of his life studying – mostly in the Reading Room of the British Museum – and

developing his theories. He wrote them in a massive book entitled *Capital*, the first volume of which was published in 1867. It was to be one of those books that have shaped history.

Marx pondered on the history of mankind so far, and tried to explain what had happened and what would happen next. He thought that man's actions have been caused by a desire for wealth, and in any historical period the really important thing to study is the production and control of wealth. At different times, according to the main sources of wealth, certain classes would dominate the others. When wealth came from the land, the feudal lords were masters. When trade became the readiest source of wealth, the middle classes (Marx used the French word *bourgeoisie*) became the masters. Now industry was

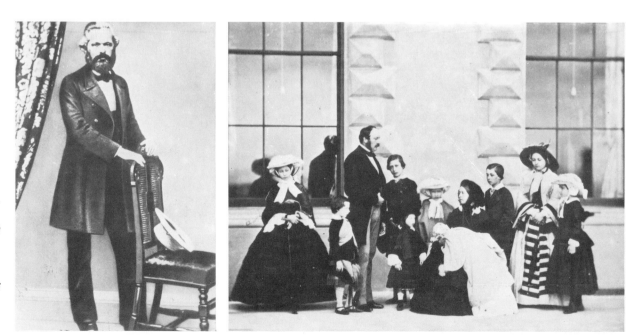

right: *Karl Marx, 1818–83, photographed in 1861.*

far right: *Victoria, 1819–1901, and Albert, 1819–61, with their children, photographed at Osborne, Isle of Wight, in 1857. From left to right the group is: Alice, Arthur, the Prince Consort, the Prince of Wales, Leopold, Louise, the Queen holding Beatrice, Alfred, the Princess Royal, Helena.*

Contemporary bird's-eye view of the Great Exhibition from the south, with the Serpentine behind it. The western half was where goods from Britain and her empire were displayed, and the eastern half was for foreign exhibitors. The iron and glass structure was 1,848 feet long and 456 feet at its widest point (563 and 139 metres).

becoming the great source of wealth, and it depended on the working class. (Marx called them *proletarians*, from the ancient Roman term for people so poor that they had nothing but their children.) Since the proletarians now had power over the main source of wealth, Marx argued, they must inevitably become the next master-class, and they would run everything in a socialist fashion.

Thus Marx saw the changes brought about by the Industrial Revolution as part of Progress, something that was bound to happen. It was like predestination, though no god was involved. There were in Britain many people who would have disagreed with Marx on everything else, including God, but had a similar feeling about Progress. The bourgeoisie themselves firmly believed in Progress. Despite the unhappy plight of the poor (and Parliament was doing more to help them than ever before) it seemed to them that everything was improving. Machines were constantly improving, making more goods, making them better, making them cheaper so that some day everybody would have sufficient. Thanks to science and engineering, streets and houses were being lit by gas, supplied with fresh running water, cleansed by means of drains and sewers. Trains and ships were becoming bigger and faster, travel easier and cheaper. British goods were wanted all over the world; wherever trade was free British firms were well in the lead. Anybody with the will to work, so it was believed, could always get on in life. Books and magazines were cheap and plentiful for those who wished to improve their minds. People who talked of 'the Hungry Forties' were looking on the dark side only.

A young queen had come to the British throne in 1837. Her name was Victoria. None could foresee it then, but she was to reign until the century was over, and give her name to that whole period of history, its ideals and prejudices, fashions and achievements. Victoria married a highly intelligent, well-educated, serious-minded German prince, Albert of Saxe-Coburg-Gotha. It was his idea, as the mid-point of the century approached, to hold a great gathering of what mankind had accomplished, an exhibition where the nations of the world could display the best of whatever they produced. On May Day of the first year of the second half of the century, the Great Exhibition would be opened.

The idea itself was original, and an equally original setting was devised for it – a vast glass palace in Hyde Park. Joseph Paxton, the Duke of Devonshire's gardener and friend, imagined an enormous greenhouse and had the organising genius to get it built in time. Prince Albert had never been popular in Britain. Many had mocked at this earnest foreigner who depended on his wife, and they ridiculed this silly scheme of his. But it proved to be Albert's triumph. It was a huge success. Visitors flocked and admired this festival of industry and peaceful trade, in which Britain was so apparently leading the world.

THE POUND AND THE SHILLING
"WHOEVER THOUGHT OF MEETING YOU HERE!"

opposite, top: **Industry and invention**: *agricultural machinery by Hornsby and Son, and an envelope-folding machine of Thomas de la Rue and Company.*

opposite, bottom: **Domestic hardware**: *a lily-shaped fitting for gas-lights (with statuette of Dorothea from 'Don Quixote') and a fireplace complete with fender.*

above: **Fine Art**: *'The Greek Slave' by the American sculptor Hiram Power. On its revolving pedestal, this life-size figure was probably the most talked-of single exhibit. A characteristic contemporary comment goes thus: 'During the early Greek revolutions the captives were exposed for sale in the Turkish bazaar, under the name of "slaves". The artist has delineated a young girl, deprived of her clothing, standing before the licentious gaze of a wealthy Eastern barbarian. Her face expresses shame and disgust at her ignominious position, while about her lip hovers that contemptuous scorn which a woman can so well show for her unmanly oppressor. It is a hard thing to produce a perfect work, and many faults were soon found to injure the well-merited reputation of the statue. The manner in which the right hand was made to lean upon the trunk of a tree, while the whole weight of the body was thrown upon the left leg was, however, the only grave error committed by the sculptor.'*

top right: *Reducing the admission charge on some days to a shilling attracted thousands of visitors who could otherwise never have thought of coming. For the first time, cheap excursions were organised by the railway companies. This is an 'Illustrated London News' drawing of Hyde Park Corner on a 'shilling day'. Below is a comment from 'Punch' on the mingling of the classes.*

right: *Keble College, Oxford, was founded in 1869 and named after a leader of the Oxford Movement. The chapel is one of the best-known works of William Butterfield, 1814–1900, a prominent Victorian Gothic architect.*

left: *Sheffield from the south-east, by William Ibbitt, 1855. On one side of the town centre the scene is dominated by rail and canal installations, and elsewhere industrial chimneys seem to be sprouting uncontrolled.*

Victoria's subjects have sometimes been criticised for being self-satisfied, and no doubt a number of them were. But they had some excuse for such a feeling when they thought about the growing wealth of Britain, and compared her peace with the revolution-racked Continent. What was the reason for Britain's comparatively happy situation? There could be several explanations.

It could have been because of what successive governments did. Free Trade was adopted – W. E. Gladstone, Chancellor of the Exchequer on various occasions after 1852, did most to reduce and abolish customs dues – and British industries got an advantage. There was a steady stream of acts which gradually improved working conditions and living conditions for the poorer classes and reduced reasons for discontent.

It could have been that, whatever the conditions, the lower classes had an innate respect for their 'betters'. Snobbery flourished; it was early in Victoria's reign that W. M. Thackeray defined and illustrated it in his *Book of Snobs*. Every Englishman, the saying went, loved a lord.

It may have been that the upper classes earned their peace. Though some of them could be dangerously slow and stupid, the British aristocracy usually had the sense to know when it was time to give in, to yield to reform demands, and to reinforce themselves by admitting new peers and squires from among the wealthiest members of the middle class. Indeed, many landowners were also mine-owners and factory-owners. It is also possible that many of the upper and middle classes deserved respect for trying honestly to live up to their ideal of how a Christian gentleman should behave.

The leaders of Victorian Britain were taught this ideal at school. This was a time when the public schools—which in fact were private and expensive—increased very rapidly in both size and number. The school which most obviously set the standard was Rugby, where Rev. Dr Thomas Arnold was headmaster from 1828 to his death in 1842. He began a trend that made the playing-field and chapel as important as the classroom. Games were no longer just a fairly harmless way of spending surplus energy, but a way to moral virtue: sportsmanship, fair play, team spirit, 'playing the game'. In the chapel the boys were taught that Christianity was a practical way of life and it was their duty to follow it. They were to be the leaders of their society; in class and out, they were

right: *The Primitive Methodist Chapel at Hetton-le-Hole, County Durham, is simple but with a few traces of eighteenth-century classical architectural tradition. The chapel itself is above, the school-room below. The building was largely built by local miners in their spare time, with stone and transport provided by the mine owner.*

labourers digging canals (they were nick-named 'navigators' or 'navvies') and then building railways. When they settled down, they naturally wanted their own churches. In some drab working towns, where men could find little pleasant to occupy their few hours of leisure, church or chapel was the main alternative to the public house. Drunkenness was common, and often led to starvation, neglect and savage beatings for the drunkard's wife and children. It was no wonder that religious people were often vehement teetotallers. On Saturday nights in some Irish districts only the local priest could restore order after the police had failed.

Many people, and not only the poor, wanted their religion to bring colour and excitement into their lives. It was still the period of the Romantic Revival, and one of the past times most popular with Romantic writers was the time of knights and castles, the Middle Ages – the very time when the Church had been at its most splendid. It all fitted together. Some members of the Church of England tried to bring into their own worship part of the dignity, ceremony and deep feeling that they believed to have existed in the medieval Church. Among these were some of the most active young minds in the University of Oxford, and their attempt to restore a high feeling of divine authority in the Church of England became known as the Oxford Movement. One or two did as their critics had suspected they would, and went over to the Roman Catholic Church; one, John Henry Newman, became a cardinal. But the others brought a new energy to what became known as the Anglican 'High Church'.

Naturally such churchmen were attracted towards the style of building that had marked the Middle Ages, Gothic, but they were not alone in this. Medieval-looking spires and pinnacles started to jut from the skyline of industrial town centres and suburbs. They belonged not only to churches of all denominations, but to town halls, museums, hotels, schools, railway stations, private houses. These buildings made full use of the materials that the Industrial Revolution had made plentiful. Bricks, usually red but sometimes yellow or blue, were now cheap everywhere, thanks to the railways, and iron was cast not only for roof-beams and pillars, but for elaborately designed ornaments and railings. Yet it may seem curious that, in a time of change and invention faster than mankind had ever known, and of confidence in Progress, people chose to revive the style of a lost age.

taught the duties of obedience and of command. For several generations every good school in Britain tried to produce young men with these qualities.

Respect for religion was equally strong amongst the ordinary people. Marx called religion 'the opium of the people' because he thought it made them dream of better times in the next world instead of struggling for more wealth and power in this. It was now about a century since the Wesleys had 'brought the church to the people' and Methodism was a great influence in the lives of very many of the working class. In every industrial town and village stood the plain chapels where the working people met to pray and hear sermons, and where some of them learned to preach and to lead. Another Church which had great influence now among the working classes was the Catholic. Irishmen had migrated in their thousands to other parts of Britain, at first as unskilled

The Crimean War and the Eastern Question

Three years after the Great Exhibition, the long peace ended. There was war between Turkey, Britain, France and Piedmont on one side, Russia on the other. The allies' problem was that which always faced any enemy of Russia: how to attack anywhere that could really damage so vast a country. The war began with Russian attacks on the Turkish Empire, but once these were resisted, the allies had few ideas about what to do next. They decided that their best objective would be the relatively warm and fertile peninsula of the Crimea, where the Tsar had at Sebastopol his main southern naval base.

Presently the British people became familiar with new names. Streets were named Alma, Balaclava, Inkerman. Warm garments were named after Lord Raglan and Lord Cardigan. The military decoration of the Victoria Cross was instituted. Florence Nightingale became famous as 'The Lady with the Lamp'. The first big war for forty years would have been interesting enough anyway, but the British public had their emotions specially stirred by reports of the miseries the soldiers had to endure, partly because of the gross incompetence of the officers and officials who organised the army. Thanks to fast communications a practical electric telegraph had been invented by the American Samuel Morse in 1832—newspapers reported promptly. In *The Times* the dispatches of war correspondent William Russell plainly exposed the stupidity and callousness of the British high command; the readers were furious, most of them at the faults of the authorities, but some at Russell for 'unpatriotically' revealing them.

This war involved the British people in a new way. Previous wars, of course, had had very important effects on their fortunes, and often enough the people had been wildly excited by victory and indignant at defeat. Now there was growing a more genuine feeling for the common soldiers, the men who previously had often been despised as crude, stupid fellows who (when they were not making Britain victorious) had to be controlled by ferocious punishment for any breach of discipline. Now the Victoria Cross was given to all ranks equally; the Romans had done this, and the French under Napoleon, but it was a new attitude for Britain. Previously, wounded soldiers had had to depend on the help of a few soldiers' wives

and assorted camp-followers for nursing, if they survived the attentions of army surgeons who were too few and often rough-and-ready. Now Miss Nightingale amazed society by taking genuine *ladies* to care for the wounded and, after the first surprise, people praised and accepted this new attitude to nursing. Though it took until 1881 for flogging to be abolished completely, and some of the old distrust of the common soldier lingered on, the Victorians were coming to look on their soldiers as fellow-citizens with feelings and rights like other human beings.

ENTHUSIASM OF PATERFAMILIAS,
On Reading the Report of the Grand Charge of British Cavalry on the 25th.

"WELL, JACK! HERE'S GOOD NEWS FROM HOME. WE'RE TO HAVE A MEDAL."
"THAT'S VERY KIND. MAYBE ONE OF THESE DAYS WE'LL HAVE A COAT TO STICK IT ON?"

Two comments from 'Punch' reveal different aspects of the British public's attitude towards the army in the Crimea.

But why was there a war, what was it about? Some, like John Bright who simply described Crimea as 'A Crime', thought that it should never have been. The main reason was the Eastern Question.

The Ottoman Turkish Empire seemed quite unable to pull itself together. After the Greek War of Independence there was a revolt by Mehemet Ali, whose Egyptians routed the Sultan's army, and the Sultan was saved only by the intervention of the European powers. They did not want the Turkish Empire to be destroyed, because that would cause all sorts of problems in balancing power afresh in the Middle East, so they forced Mehemet Ali to retreat to Egypt. Tsar Nicholas I, considering how weak and inefficient the Sultan's government obviously was, thought that the Ottoman Empire was falling to pieces anyway. He called it 'the sick man of Europe' and suggested that the powers ought to make arrangements about sharing out the estate when the invalid passed away.

The Tsar may have been right, but the other powers were well aware that any share-out would make Russia bigger still. Russia already had an old claim to protect all the Sultan's Christian subjects (page 30), and there were now the beginnings of what could grow into an even more disturbing claim. Russia was by far the greatest of the Slav nations, and some Slavs of other nations believed that all Slavs should work together (page 58). This could make Russia the leader of all the people of eastern Europe. If the Slav peoples of the Balkans were freed from Turkish rule, would they naturally become clients of Russia? As what was called the Pan-Slav Movement became more important during the later part of the nineteenth century, this question was to grow in importance.

Apart from the general distrust of Russian intentions, Britain had a special worry, the possible threat to her eastern trade. If Russia were to take Constantinople and the Dardanelles, she could not only close the Black Sea to all other shipping, but could move her fleets in and out of the Mediterranean at will. In fact, most Russian statesmen did not want Constantinople, because they realised what hostility this would provoke against Russia; all they wanted was for the straits to be declared neutral, so that their ships and other people's could move freely. But Britain remained suspicious about the intentions of 'the Russian Bear'.

France, with considerably less to worry about in the

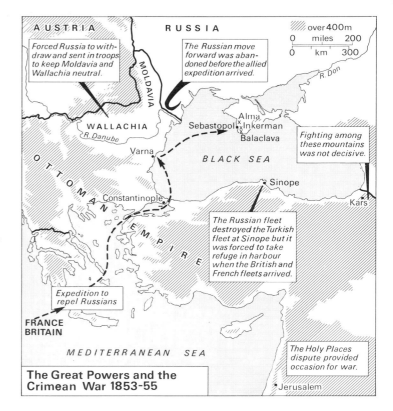

AUSTRIA RUSSIA

over 400m
0 miles 200
0 km 300

Forced Russia to withdraw and sent in troops to keep Moldavia and Wallachia neutral.

The Russian move forward was abandoned before the allied expedition arrived.

MOLDAVIA
R. Don

WALLACHIA
R. Danube

Sebastopol Alma Inkerman
Balaclava

Varna

Fighting among these mountains was not decisive.

BLACK SEA

Sinope

Kars

Constantinople

OTTOMAN EMPIRE

The Russian fleet destroyed the Turkish fleet at Sinope but it was forced to take refuge in harbour when the British and French fleets arrived.

Expedition to repel Russians

FRANCE
BRITAIN

MEDITERRANEAN SEA

The Holy Places dispute provided occasion for war.

The Great Powers and the Crimean War 1853-55

Jerusalem

Middle East, brought on the war. Napoleon III was still new and looking for popularity. He claimed to be the protector of all *Catholic* Christians in Turkey, and argued that Catholic monks were entitled to certain rights in looking after the Holy Places in and near Jerusalem. The Sultan did not want trouble, and agreed. But the Tsar took this as a blow to his own prestige, because it weakened the rights of the Orthodox monks whom he protected. So he put pressure upon the unfortunate Sultan. France promised the Sultan support, so this time he stood firm. Russia increased her pressure by moving troops into the principalities of Moldavia and Wallachia and, after long diplomatic negotiations had failed to settle matters, Turkey declared war on Russia in October 1853. Napoleon III had a promise to keep, wanted to go on pleasing the Catholics, and thought that it would be good for his reputation if he could avenge Napoleon I's disaster of 1812. The British government thought that it was necessary to prop up Turkey. France and Britain therefore declared war on Russia in March 1854.

The Congress of Paris modified the laws of the sea at a time when shipping was changing more fundamentally than ever before, from sail and wood to steam and iron. This contemporary print shows the 'Great Britain' sailing from Liverpool for Australia in August 1852. Designed by the brilliant engineer I. K. Brunel, 1806-59, and launched in 1843, she was propelled by a screw and sails; during her active life the mast and sail plan were altered more than once. On this voyage she carried 630 passengers and a crew of 138. The tug at her side relies on paddles while the ship in the distance has sails only.

Sardinia–Piedmont joined the war in January 1855. She had little interest in Turkey or Russia, but wanted to earn the friendship of France and to be a member of the international conference which must surely come at the end of the war. Piedmont, in fact, was trying to find support for a future war that had nothing to do with the Crimea.

With three of the five Great Powers involved, there was an obvious danger that the war could spread to all. But Austria and Prussia both stayed out, and agreed to support each other if either were attacked. Because he had helped Austria in 1849 the Tsar thought that he could rely on some friendship in return, but instead Austria made it very clear that she was going to stop Russia from becoming any stronger in the Danube area. The allies at last succeeded in taking Sebastopol in September 1855, but this brought them no nearer inflicting real damage on Russia. In fact the war was a stalemate, and could have dragged on and on. But Austria threatened to join the allies if Russia would not make peace. The result was a peace conference held in Paris in March 1856.

The peace treaty turned out to be as indecisive as the war had been. Russia gave up her claim to protect the Christians in Turkey and withdrew her troops from the mouth of the Danube. The Danube was to be free, open to the ships of all nations, and the Black Sea was to be neutral – Russia promised not to keep any warships there. Meanwhile the Sultan promised that all his subjects could worship as they pleased and that Christians could hold government posts. He also promised reforms in the law, including the abolition of torture. *If* all these promises could be carried out, *perhaps* the 'sick man' might become healthy and there would be no more Eastern Question.

The statesmen at the Congress of Paris tried to do more than just end a war. They attempted to improve international affairs generally, and agreed on certain rules to protect merchant shipping on the high seas. Privateering was abolished, and there were severe restrictions placed on the right of warships to interfere with neutral ships trading to enemy ports. Though in past wars Britain had suffered from

French and American privateers, there was no doubt that she gave up more than she gained in this agreement. The Royal Navy at this time was much stronger than any rivals so these rules would hinder it and reduce its advantage. But it was all in the interests of more free trade, and this suited the 'workshop of the world'.

As a war, the Crimean may seem to have decided nothing. It is remembered for famous blunders, like the Charge of the Light Brigade at Balaclava and the fog-blinded infantry onslaught at Inkerman, and perhaps the whole war was itself a blunder. It is important as a turning-point, though. After the long peace, great powers had begun again to use war in the old game of international power politics.

The French Second Empire

The 1851 Exhibition had proclaimed unmistakably that Britain led Europe and the world in industry and commerce. Napoleon III was determined that, under him, France would lead in every other way. He knew that, if his Second Empire was to last longer than the past few systems of government in France, he had to keep the French people as a whole on his side. It was not easy, because there were so many parties with widely different beliefs, from the most reactionary royalists to the most revolutionary republicans. But they all had one thing in common: they were French. If he could copy his uncle in making France glorious, Napoleon III might earn the loyalty of the entire people. (Though he must take care not to suffer the defeats his uncle had suffered at the end.)

His intervention at Rome (page 65) pleased Catholics (but not liberals) and it was a military victory eventually, and a diplomatic success over the Austrians who would rather have done the job themselves.

The Crimean War also had its religious side, had more spectacular fighting, and ended with the French Emperor being host to a grand congress in Paris.

Napoleon III's next war was calculated to buy him the approval of his more liberal subjects. As a young man, Louis Napoleon had been a friend of Italian revolutionaries, but since he had come to power he seemed to have turned against them. One Italian so detested this apparent betrayal that he tried to kill Napoleon with a bomb. Another form of persuasion was practised by Count Cavour, the chief minister of Sardinia–Piedmont. He was the man who had brought his country into the Crimean War, and used his chance at the Paris Congress to try to turn the opinions of other important European statesmen against Austria. He managed to persuade Napoleon that the great French army would have no difficulty in driving the Austrians from northern Italy. Then he provoked Austria into attacking Sardinia–Piedmont, and the French came to the rescue.

The French and Piedmontese did win two great battles, Magenta and Solferino, on 4 and 24 June 1859. But they were costly victories. This was the first time Napoleon III had actually seen what war was like, and he was appalled at the suffering which was the price of glory. The Austrian army was still strong, and there were reports that other powers would intervene if France tried to push her success too far. So he made peace. Piedmont got Milan and Lombardy, but Cavour was disgruntled because he had expected Venetia as well. As a reward for her help, France received Savoy and Nice from Piedmont. It was said that the people of both areas were more French than Italian, and when a plebiscite was held there the majority voted for France. One native of Nice who did not regard it as French was Giuseppe Garibaldi.

There was another man who had seen the slaughter at Solferino, and he determined that something must be done to

Solferino: French infantry attacking over ground already strewn with dead and wounded. The artist may or may not have witnessed such a charge, but he obviously understood the cost in casualties.

mitigate the horrible effects of war. He was a Swiss named Henri Dunant, and he went back to his city of Geneva to seek support; he wanted international agreement and an organisation to relieve suffering. He was successful. The city of Geneva invited governments to send representatives to a meeting in the autumn of 1863 to discuss the matter, and fourteen, including the main European states, accepted the invitation. At the conference all but two agreed to sign what has become famous as the Geneva Convention. Over the years, the governments of most states in the world were to add their signatures. In addition to the international organisation, national branches were set up. All of them, except where religious reasons prevented the use of what might have been seen as a Christian symbol, honoured Dunant by taking as their badge the Swiss flag with colours reversed: on a white background, a red cross.

During the 1860s Napoleon III's laurels began to droop. He tried to set up the Austrian emperor's brother, Maximilian, as Emperor of Mexico, but when most of the Mexicans resisted and the United States threatened he withdrew his troops. Maximilian refused to flee, and was shot by the Mexican republicans. After this ignominious venture Napoleon kept his soldiers at home. He was ageing and ill. But he still wanted the rest of Europe to show respect to France, and knew that his people expected him to make sure of it.

Did the French approve of Napoleon III's actions? He took no chances. Newspapers were not allowed to criticise, the Assembly had no real power to change the law or advise the government, and, to make extra sure, the voters' lists and election results were 'rigged' so that the emperor's supporters got huge majorities. But were these corrupt methods necessary? France had had plenty of time to cool down after the turmoil of 1848, and most of the people seemed to be quite content with the Empire. Perhaps these methods were doing more harm than good, because they certainly gave Napoleon's enemies the chance to call him crooked, cowardly and weak. One of his most violent critics was the famous novelist and poet Victor Hugo who, from his safe retreat in Guernsey, inveighed against the great Napoleon's unworthy successor, 'Napoleon the Little'.

The emperor decided to 'liberalise'. Censorship of the press was relaxed. The Assembly was allowed to criticise government ministers and to suggest new laws. Elections became more honest. As a result, more opposition members were elected and there were some scathing attacks on the government in some newspapers, but on the whole the 'Liberal

right: *Napoleon III's efforts to inspire awe did not always impress. This was the reaction in 'Punch' at a time when he appeared to be threatening Britain.*

far right: *Henri Dunant, 1828–1910, whose writings led to the formation of the Red Cross.*

PUNCH, OR THE LONDON CHARIVARI—November 19, 1859.

BOW-WOW !!

Empire' policy was a success. Most of the Assembly and, as far as anyone could tell, most of France firmly supported Napoleon III.

The Second Empire had to have a suitable capital. Paris was partly rebuilt, and gained the reputation that it was to keep for many years: 'the gay city', *la ville lumière*, the Mecca of artists and millionaires, the home of fashion and of everything smart and expensive. The face of Paris was transfigured most by the wide boulevards laid out by Baron Hausmann, with the emperor himself taking a close interest; they were splendid for strolling and shopping, but they would also give the artillery splendid fields of fire if revolutionaries tried to take to the streets again. That was still a real danger. The government did not need to worry very much about discontent among industrial workers, because these were still very few in comparison with the rural population. But Paris could still be explosive, with its traditions of revolution, its crowded poor, and its cliques of clever talkers and writers who were not impressed and were sharply critical. Paris invariably elected opposition members to the Assembly. The people of Paris were definitely not admirers of Napoleon III. Yet, whenever

the Second Empire is mentioned nowadays, people automatically think of Paris as its symbol, almost as its heart; they think of the boulevards and cafés, the Place de l'Opera, the operettas of Jacques Offenbach and the 'shocking' *can-can*.

And how different from the London of good Queen Victoria!

It is because this picture of Paris is firmly fixed that we must always bear in mind that Paris was not France.

above: *This air view of the Place de l'Etoile (Star) shows clearly how well the streets were planned for several different purposes.*

left: *The fashionable crowd in the Boulevard des Italiens, 1856. A lithograph by E. Guerard.*

5 New powers and old

In the third quarter of the nineteenth century Europe took on a new appearance. The era of revolutions was over; it had ended in failure. From now on liberals and nationalists generally worked with the governments of their states instead of trying to overthrow them, while the governments often found that by agreeing to liberal reforms and encouraging nationalism and adapting it they could make their states stronger, not weaker. So the time of revolutions gave way to a time when Europe was dominated by a few great states, most of them nation-states, with powerful governments.

These were not the same Great Powers as before. Between the late 1850s and the early 1870s there were dramatic events that transformed them all, in one way or another, and created the pattern of European states which would have to face the tremendous problems of the next century. It is important to learn how each of these Great Powers took shape.

The Kingdom of Italy

Between 1820 and 1849 many Italians had died in plots and risings intended to bring freedom to their people and some-times to unite all Italy. We cannot tell what most of the Italian people thought. What did they understand by 'freedom'? Were they more interested in earning a decent livelihood? Did they care about Italy as a whole, or only about their own part of it? Whatever the answers, it does seem likely that the repeated revolts aroused sympathy, because they made the governments seem more and more police-minded and oppressive, while imprisoned or dead rebels seemed noble martyrs.

Heroism alone, however, was not going to succeed. This was obvious by the 1850s. The Austrian army was strong enough to put down any revolts, and even when the army of Sardinia–Piedmont had helped in 1848 it had proved too weak. Therefore Count Cavour, as we saw on page 77, contrived to enlist French help and in 1859 gained much of northern Italy for Piedmont. At the same time the liberals in several other Italian states seized this opportunity, rose, and joined their states to the Piedmontese kingdom. As the map shows,

Garibaldi landing at Marsala, 1860.

Sardinia-Piedmont thus suddenly expanded to cover most of the northern half of Italy. Some liberals may have reflected sourly that this looked more like the expansion of one kingdom than the liberation of a people, but none could deny that Cavour's diplomatic scheming had worked where all the plots and risings had failed.

The year 1860 was Garibaldi's. He was once described in this way: 'Heart of gold, head of an ox'. Perhaps 'bull' would better have suggested his headlong valour. In 1859, as in 1848, Garibaldi had raised a force of volunteers that had scored daring successes against the Austrians. Now, because he simply thought that the liberation of Italy was a matter of fighting again and again, wherever a bad or a foreign government ruled over Italians, he planned to drive the French from Nice, his birthplace, which they had been given as a reward for their aid in 1859. A fight with France was the last thing Cavour and the Piedmontese government wanted. They managed to point Garibaldi in another direction by showing him a place where a far bigger population needed liberating. In May, with 1,000 red-shirted volunteers, Garibaldi sailed for Sicily.

Thanks partly to unofficial protection quietly given by British warships, Garibaldi and his 'Thousand' landed safely on 11 May and began an astonishing career through the island. Four days later they defeated the royal troops at Calatafimi. A fortnight later Garibaldi occupied Palermo and set up a new government. In two months he held the whole island. In August, again with British warships helpfully sailing near, he crossed to the mainland. He entered the city of Naples on 7 September. He made ready to finish off the royal army and then move on to liberate the Papal States.

The exploits of Garibaldi and his gallant Thousand (now very much enlarged) thrilled newspaper readers everywhere. Even cool Cavour was pleased, for he calculated that the people of Sicily and Naples would vote to join the Kingdom of Sardinia-Piedmont. But an attack on Rome would ruin everything, for it would mean a battle with the French garrison there. Garibaldi refused to stop. His heart told him that there were Italians waiting to be liberated, and he must do it. Somehow Cavour had to forestall him. He did it by sending the Piedmontese army into the Papal States from the north, with orders to march through to Naples but to keep to the east, well away from Rome. The Pope's own small army

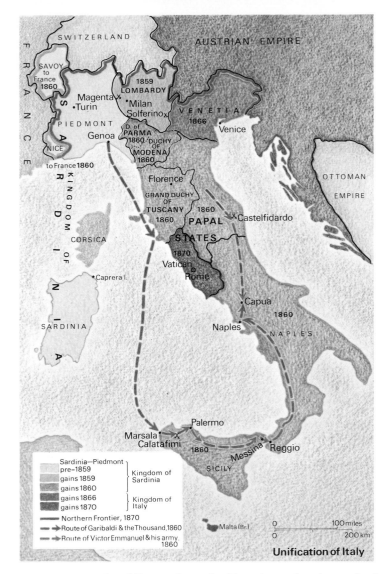

Unification of Italy

(which was quite different from the French garrison) marched across to stop the Piedmontese and was scattered at Castelfidardo. The Piedmontese came to Naples. The king himself, Victor Emmanuel II, was with his army. In person he congratulated Garibaldi on his glorious achievements. Then he asked him to go no farther. Disappointed but loyal, Garibaldi obeyed.

Votes were taken in Naples and Sicily, and also in those

81

parts of the Papal States which the Piedmontese army had occupied. As expected, they all chose to join Sardinia–Piedmont. Now that so much of the peninsula was under one crown, it made sense to change the name to Kingdom of Italy. This was proclaimed on 17 March 1861. Victor Emmanuel was king and Florence was chosen as the most convenient city to be capital. Cavour, who had done so much to bring this about, died in June, aged 52.

Venetia was still held by Austria. In 1866 there came the opportunity of allying with another strong power against Austria. This time the ally was Prussia. In the 1866 war the Italian army and navy were beaten by the Austrians, but Prussia won the war by victories elsewhere. So, in the peace settlement, Italy got Venetia.

Still the Kingdom of Italy lacked its natural capital, Rome. More than once during the 1860s Garibaldi, from the little island of Caprera where he had made his home, tried to seize Rome, but he was stopped either by the Italian army or – this

Victor Emmanuel II; born 1820, King of Sardinia 1849, King of Italy 1861, died 1878. He was sometimes known as 'the gallant king'.

time with heavy losses – by the French garrison. It was in 1870, and again because of foreign politics, that Italy's chance came. In that year France was at war with Germany, and far too deeply in trouble to bother about Rome. So the Italian army was able to take over without fuss, and at last Rome was the capital of united Italy.

The Pope still presented a serious problem. His position depended on arguments which were at least as old as the Middle Ages, and as valid and relevant as ever. Could the head of a universal Church, in which politics and nationality should have no significance, be subject to any earthly ruler? Wisely, the Italian government did not push its success to the limit. The Pope was left with a small area around the Vatican Palace which was not part of the Kingdom of Italy. Vatican City was recognised as an independent state, though it was not until 1929 that the Pope recognised the Kingdom of Italy. It may be that the loss of the Papal States was a blessing in disguise for the Church. It freed the Pope from having to spend part of his time as an Italian prince, mixed up in politics; from now on the Pope could speak with more purely religious and moral power throughout the world.

The unification of Italy has understandably seemed to many people a noble cause. After long years of struggle and sacrifice, a great and gifted people living in a land of romantic beauty won freedom and unity. In Italian it is called the *risorgimento*, resurrection. Was this the truth? It may well have been the vision of men like Garibaldi, and it may well have become a belief to inspire future Italian patriots. But there is another way of looking at it. When the revolutionaries had all failed, what succeeded were old-fashioned diplomacy and power politics used, very skilfully, by an existing government.

The German Empire

In 1848, when liberals seemed to have won over everybody in Germany, the Prussian Assembly voted a liberal constitution for the kingdom. Only two members voted against. One was Otto von Bismarck, a country squire or *Junker*. He believed in God and the king, and had no time for liberals and nationalists with their windy speeches about freedom, unity and the people. Long afterwards he said to another Prussian Assembly: 'Place in the hands of the King of Prussia the strongest possible military power, and he will be able to carry out the policy you wish; this policy cannot succeed through speeches and festivals and songs, it can only be carried out through blood and iron.' His own determination was iron, but at the same time he was sensitive, emotional sometimes to the point of tears, and imaginative. Such qualities combined with his great intelligence to make him a very formidable politician.

In 1849, when Frederick William refused the crown offered by the Frankfurt Parliament, Bismarck was relieved. He had feared that Prussia might merge into a flabby united Germany. What he wanted was Prussia to grow stronger until, if Germany should unite, it would be on Prussia's terms and under Prussia's control.

During the 1850s Bismarck became one of the best-known politicians in Prussia, and represented his king in the Diet of the restored Germanic Confederation. Here he tried to wipe out the memory of Prussia's humiliation (page 63) by behaving as if he were the equal of the Austrian chairman and taking every opportunity to show that the Diet could not accomplish anything unless Prussia agreed. Slowly Prussia's prestige was rebuilt. Meanwhile the German customs union, the Zollverein, continued to prosper, still under the leadership of Prussia.

In 1861 William I became King of Prussia. He and Bismarck quickly sensed that they could trust each other, and the king appointed Bismarck his chief minister. Though most members of the Prussian Assembly disapproved, he increased the army; he was not responsible to the Assembly, only to the king. When newspapers criticised him, he clapped on new censorship laws. He cared little for popularity, though he knew that he would become popular enough if his plans succeeded.

Outside Prussia itself, Bismarck had to consider three likely obstacles to Prussia dominating Germany. Firstly, of course, Austria would not give up her place. Secondly, many of the smaller German states disliked and feared Prussia. Thirdly, other powers might be concerned about any alteration of the balance, and the French Second Empire was both a near neighbour and in the habit of interfering in the affairs of other countries. Bismarck made ready to seize any opportunity to overcome these obstacles, and he did it with such skill that many people believed that he brought about the ensuing series of events by his own Machiavellian cunning.

In 1864 the Danish king was foolish enough to break his promises over Schleswig and Holstein, and to incorporate the Duchies into Denmark. Both Austria and Prussia moved promptly to maintain the treaty and to act as defenders of the German inhabitants of the Duchies. They soon defeated Denmark, and arranged to administer Schleswig and Holstein themselves. The arrangement was so badly drawn up, however, that arguments about it were bound to arise.

In 1866 a dispute duly arose, and both Austria and Prussia were ready for a show-down. The smaller German states mostly took Austria's side, but Bismarck had more success abroad. Italy, as we have seen would always gladly fight, against Austria. Russia had not forgotten Austrian 'ingratitude' at the time of the Crimean War (page 76), and Bismarck had taken care to be very helpful to the Tsar's government during a Polish revolt in 1863. So Russia would be a friendly neutral. As for France, Napoleon III had made secret agreements with both Austria and Prussia to the effect that France would get 'compensation', whichever side won; so he sat back and waited for the reward of his cleverness.

Otto von Bismarck, 1815–98, portrayed by Lenbach in the 1890s. He has sometimes been nicknamed 'the iron chancellor'.

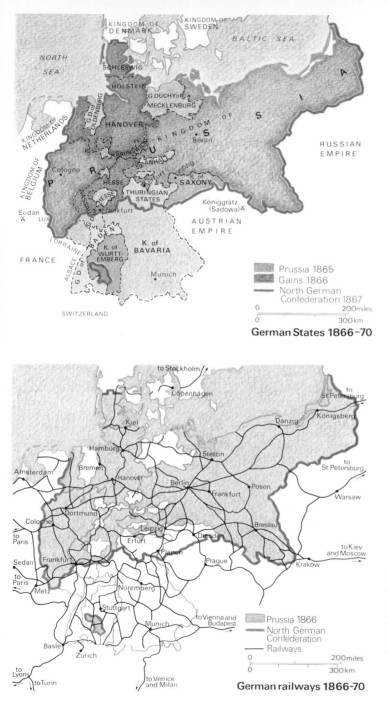

KINGDOM OF
DENMARK

KINGDOM OF
SWEDEN

BALTIC SEA

NORTH
SEA

SCHLESWIG

HOLSTEIN

G.DUCHYof
MECKLENBURG

G.Dof
OLDENBURG

KINGDOM OF
NETHERLANDS

HANOVER

RUSSIAN
EMPIRE

KINGDOM OF
BELGIUM

Cologne

P R U S S I A

Berlin

BRUNSWICK

ANHALT

K of
SAXONY

HESSE

ERFURT

LEIPZIG

NASSAU

HESSE

THURINGIAN
STATES

Sedan
X

LUX

Frankfurt

Koniggratz
(Sadowa) X

AUSTRIAN
EMPIRE

LORRAINE

BADEN

G.Dof

K of
WURT-
EMBERG

K. of
BAVARIA

FRANCE

ALSACE

Munich

Prussia 1865
Gains 1866
North German
Confederation 1867

0   200miles
0   300km

SWITZERLAND

German States 1866-70

to Stockholm

to Copenhagen

to
St Petersburg

Kiel

Danzig

Königsberg

Hamburg

Bremen

Stettin

Amsterdam

to
St Petersburg

Hanover

Berlin

Posen

Warsaw

Dortmund

Frankfurt

Cologne

to Paris

Leipzig

Breslau

Erfurt

Dresden

to Kiev
and Moscow

Sedan

Plauen

to Paris

Frankfurt

Prague

Krakow

Metz

Nuremberg

Stuttgart

to Vienna and
Budapest

Prussia 1866
North German
Confederation
Railways

Basle

Munich

Zurich

0   200miles
0   300km

to
Lyons

to Turin

to Venice
and Milan

German railways 1866-70

The Austro–Prussian War of 1866 is often called the Seven Weeks' War. Prussia won with startling speed. The decisive battle was on 3 July at Königgrätz, or Sadowa, in Bohemia, where Prussian armies converged on the main Austrian army. In the peace that followed, Bismarck was very kind to Austria, which lost only Venetia, and that to Italy. He did not want Austria to have any reason for seeking revenge, and trying to regain territory from Prussia. Prussia took her prizes elsewhere. Some smaller states, including Hanover and Frankfurt, became part of Prussia. The Germanic Confederation was dissolved. In its place there was a new North German Confederation, in which Prussia was by far the biggest partner and the constitution was drawn up so as to make it easy for Prussia to dominate the rest. The south German states were left to form their own association if they wished, provided that Austria did not become a member.

The war is also occasionally known as the Needle-Gun War, after the Prussian rifle. It was the first practical breech-loader used as a standard weapon by any army in the world. Though far from perfect, it was much quicker and handier than the muzzle-loaders being employed by the other armies. The Prussian high command had also relied on railways to get their men to the right place at the right time. This, with the new weapon, may suggest that the Prussians won because they were learning faster than the others how to use the Industrial Revolution in warfare. In fact many new ideas had already been tried out in the American Civil War of 1861–5, and the Prussian success owed a good deal to luck, but it was this war which made Europeans realise that steam and machines were as much matters for the soldier as for the industrialist.

Napoleon III wanted his 'compensation'. At different times he suggested to Prussia that France should be given part of the Rhineland, or allowed to take Luxemburg or even Belgium. Each time Bismarck either avoided giving a direct answer, or flatly refused. The French government felt cheated and insulted, and a feeling spread that it was time to show the upstart Prussians that France was still the foremost military power. The French army was issued with the *chassepot* rifle, a new breech-loader better than the needle-gun, and the *mitrailleuse*, a type of volley-gun which could pour out 175 bullets per minute. The Prussians meanwhile were hastily replacing their artillery with new cannon from the Krupp factories.

84

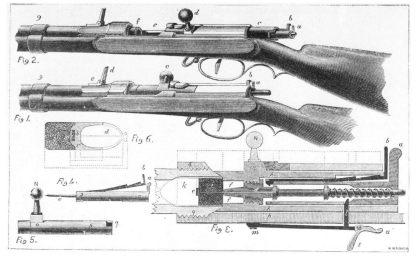

The Prussian needle-gun, a plate from Beeton's Boy's Annual, 1868. Figures 1 and 2 show the breech closed and open, Figure 3 is a section of the mechanism showing the bolt in its forward position and the needle, released by the trigger, plunged into the cartridge. Figures 4, 5 and 6 show parts of the bolt and a section through the cartridge.

In 1870 France and Prussia became involved in a complicated diplomatic wrangle. Spain wanted a new king, and the Spanish government invited a prince of the Prussian royal family, the Hohenzollerns, to accept the crown. France, unhappy at the prospect of having to face Hohenzollerns on both Rhine and Pyrenees, protested. King William of Prussia quietly asked the prince to withdraw. Bismarck and his friends among the Prussian generals were disappointed, for they had seen this as a good opportunity to have the war that would have to be fought some day. Then the French government, not content with having got what it wanted, sent an ambassador to ask King William to apologise and promise that it would never happen again. The king, who was on holiday at Ems at the time, refused, and sent a telegram telling Bismarck what had happened. This was the chance Bismarck needed. He told the newspapers, but gave them the text of the telegram with some words omitted, so that it sounded as if the interview between king and ambassador had been rude on both sides. The result was all that Bismarck could have hoped. There was indignation throughout both Prussia and France, and on 19 July France declared war on Prussia.

Because of this affair of the Ems Telegram, as it is known, Bismarck has been given the credit, or blame, for bringing about the war of 1870. But the French government, the newspapers and the people of Paris were all eager for war. They expected excitement and glory. One man who wanted

neither was Napoleon III, but he dared not refuse to fight when his subjects clamoured.

France had hoped that the southern German states would take this opportunity of bringing down Prussia, but instead they rallied behind Prussia against France. The famous French army turned out to have gay uniforms, good weapons, brave soldiers and useless leaders. The Germans proved to be bold, resourceful and extremely well led. Every battle was a French defeat until on 2 September Napoleon III and his army, trapped against the Belgian frontier at Sedan, had to surrender. For two centuries France had enjoyed the reputation of being the foremost military power in Europe; now, with shocking suddenness, the myth was exploded.

In Paris a republic was proclaimed, and some thought that they could put the blame for everything on Napoleon III. Since the Second Empire no longer existed, would the Germans now please go home? Bismarck had no such intention. This was not merely a war between governments, but between nations, and the French would have to pay.

Paris was besieged in mid-September by a Prussian army which was less numerous than the defenders. Other German armies spread steadily over northern France. New French armies were raised but, ill-trained as they were, could not turn the tide. Paris endured a winter of hardship and starvation, but surrendered on 28 January 1871.

Ten days before the surrender of Paris a ceremony had taken

place at Versailles. It was in the Hall of Mirrors of the palace of Louis XIV, whose aggressions were not forgotten by Germans. Here the German kings and princes invited William of Prussia to become emperor, and he accepted. As there had already been one German Empire, the one called Holy Roman, this was the second. It prevents confusion if we use the German word for empire, and call this the Second Reich.

The constitution of the Reich was very similar to that which had been tried out in the North German Confederation. The different states kept their own governments for local matters, but foreign relations and the armed forces were under the imperial government. The emperor (*Kaiser* in German) was commander-in-chief, and the chief minister of the empire, the chancellor, was responsible to him and not to any sort of assembly. The Reich did have a parliament, however, and this had two houses.

The upper house consisted of representatives appointed by the governments of the different states, fifty-eight all told. The bigger the state, the more representatives it had, and Prussia, the largest, had seventeen of the fifty-eight, which gave Prussia a good chance of usually being able to collect enough

extra votes to have a majority. Further, the constitution could not be altered if fourteen or more disagreed, so Prussia could always prevent the Reich from changing.

The lower house, or *Reichstag*, had 397 members, representing equal-sized constituencies covering the whole empire. Every German had a vote, and the voting was by secret ballot. This seemed all very liberal, but in fact the Reichstag had little real power. For instance, the Reichstag could vote the imperial government its income, but the contributions from the different states to the army had been fixed in the constitution, and could not be touched.

So Bismarck united Germany in his own fashion. Prussia could always direct the rest. The Reichstag, representing the German people, could talk and vote about laws, but when it came to taking action, the power lay with the emperor and his chancellor. Bismarck was chancellor.

This was not the sort of Germany that the liberals had wanted, but it may have seemed good to most of the German people. During the next twenty years Bismarck, while doing all he could to prevent liberals or socialists gaining support in the newspapers or the Reichstag, tried to show that the

The proclamation of William I as German Emperor in the Hall of Mirrors, Versailles, on 18 January 1871, painted by Anton von Werner. At the foot of the dais, facing his sovereign, stands Bismarck in white cuirassier uniform with the other great architect of victory, General Helmuth von Moltke, on his left.

ordinary people were better treated in the Second Reich than anywhere else in the world. In 1883 there was a national insurance scheme for sickness, in 1884 for accidents, and in 1889 old age pensions were introduced. At the same time German industries began to grow at a very fast rate, and the Reich was obviously prosperous and rich.

Many, probably most, of the German people were very proud of their Reich, and more so when they thought of the sweeping victories of 1870 which had inspired their leaders to create it. German writers claimed that in the war the German people had proved themselves superior. They had won over-whelmingly because they were more intelligent, better educated, had a higher sense of duty and honour, were cleaner, healthier and stronger. The nation was being identified with the army, quite reasonably since the army was largely made up of conscripts. War was not only a game of skill between governments and their professional fighters. It was becoming a contest of people against people, each pledging all their resources, moral and material, their technical skill and industrial power, to prove themselves right and mighty.

So the people gloried in their power, and the German nation was not by any means the only one to feel like this.

The Krupp steel works, founded at Essen in 1811, employed 60 workers in 1830, 8,400 in 1879 and 15,500 in 1880. Despite the fame of his guns Alfred Krupp, 1812-87, thought that his most important discovery was the seamless steel railway tire, and adopted three of these, interlocked, as his trademark; it became famous all over the world. The photographs date from 1870-80.

above left: *Steel wheels and tires ready to be fitted together*
left: *Spring workshop*
above right: *Workshop for rolling strip steel*

The French Third Republic

On 1 March 1871 the new French republican government accepted Bismarck's terms. France handed over to Germany five million francs and the two provinces of Alsace and Lorraine which had been taken from the Holy Roman Empire two centuries before. Bismarck had granted a truce so that there could be elections for a National Assembly which would have the authority to agree to this peace treaty. The Assembly met at Versailles. Though it was the sovereign body in the republic, most of its members were not republicans; about one third would have liked to bring back the Bourbon kings, and another third were for the House of Orleans. Their leader was Thiers, the man of 1830. He was still Orleanist, but was prepared to put up with a republic as the best compromise for the time being. It was not a very hopeful start for the Third Republic.

Feelings were turbulent in Paris. There most of the people were firmly republican and mistrusted the Assembly. They were bitter about their sufferings during the siege and furious that the German army had been permitted to parade in triumph along the boulevards. In March a group of republicans took charge. They set up a *commune* or town council to rule Paris. The National Guard (the Germans had let them keep their weapons when they disarmed the regular French troops) manned the defences of the city. It was difficult to know what the *communards* wanted, because there were all sorts of opinions among them, from the moderate and peaceful to the extreme and violent. But they were all against the National Assembly. Thiers and his government were not prepared to tolerate defiance. It was the old story of revolutionary Paris against conservative France. Thiers sent in the French army.

'Bloody Week' was 21 to 28 May 1871. The communards, unskilful but obstinate, defended their barricades desperately. Casualties were heavy. As the troops forced their way forward some of the communards shot hostages they had taken. The government forces exacted heavy retribution; it is not known how many thousand communards were shot during the fighting and afterwards. The commune was destroyed. But among would-be revolutionaries all over the world it became a legend of how the heroic people had been slaughtered by the hireling soldiers of a bourgeois government, and in France it

left a tradition of hatred between political parties that even the 'June Days' of 1848 had not produced.

During the early 1870s a constitution for the Third Republic was gradually pieced together. In some ways it was a contrast with the Second Reich. In France the most powerful element

above: *Communard barricades at the Pont d'Arcole and the Quai Pelletier.*

left: *Revenge! Poster advertising a journal, about 1880, The German helmet in the foreground ensures that there can be no doubt about the meaning.*

was the lower house, the Chamber of Deputies; all Frenchmen were entitled to vote in the elections of deputies. The upper house was called the Senate, and its members were mainly appointed by local councils. The president was appointed by both houses, and had very little power.

This system certainly gave most power to the deputies elected by the mass of Frenchmen (though not, of course, women) but there was a price to be paid for weakening the men at the top. Between 1873 and 1888 there were nineteen different governments, and for the rest of the century the Third Republic was constantly scandalised by cases of corruption and even treason among politicians. At this time France was the only one of the European Great Powers to be a republic, and it was not a very happy or successful example.

Disagreeing over many things, the French could agree on one. Some day there would be *revanche*, revenge on the Germans.

The Austro–Hungarian Dual Monarchy

It was easy to see that France, Germany and Italy were in some ways new powers in the early 1870s, but the two empires farther east appeared to go on very much in their old ways. Though they looked very conservative, however, Austria and Russia were not rigid and brittle.

Vienna was to Danubian Europe what Paris was to Atlantic Europe and America. It was the centre of everything elegant and fashionable. Around its medieval centre and its baroque churches and palaces there now ran the Ring, a broad thoroughfare on the site where fortifications had once stood. Here the strollers and the carriages moved against a background of stately and grandiose buildings. Some of these were famous theatres. Vienna was still the musical capital of the world, and not only for symphony and grand opera; this was the age of the Strauss family, the kings of waltz and operetta.

One of the many splendid buildings on the Ring was the Opera House, shown here in an 1873 lithograph by Franz Alt.

It has often been said that behind the brightness and charm the Habsburg monarchy was mentally dead, incapable of solving its problems and doomed to collapse. But the defeats by France and Prussia in 1859 and 1866 looked more staggering than they were, and they did in fact help by jolting the government so that it went on experimenting to find an acceptable way of ruling its very mixed collection of subjects.

At first after 1848 it had tried to impose the same firm rule on all parts of the empire, enforced by German-speaking officials. This attempt to iron out all differences did not succeed in making people forget their national feelings; instead it made them stronger.

After 1859 there was a system of provincial assemblies and an imperial assembly, but these had little real power, and anyway the voting regulations gave a disproportionate number of seats to the German-speaking middle class.

The 1866 defeat brought about more change. The Hungarians had been loud in criticising the previous systems, and arguing that they were so important that they ought to have a special position in the empire; but they had not tried to take advantage of Austria's troubles by rising in 1866. So now the imperial government decided that it would be wise to trust the Hungarians and give them what they wanted. The Habsburg Empire was divided into two, each part with its own government and assembly. One half was the Kingdom of Hungary, the other the Empire of Austria. Each half was to look after its own affairs, except that they both combined for foreign policy and war, and they had the same monarch. Francis Joseph was both emperor and king.

With both of the governments in the Dual Monarchy responsible to elected assemblies, the system may have appeared rather liberal. In practice this constitution allowed the German–Austrians to run one half, the Magyars the other. It meant that the two strongest nations were now in partnership, and this kept the Dual Monarchy quiet and apparently peaceful.

The Slav nations especially felt slighted and cheated. The Czechs, for example, who considered themselves as ancient and civilised as the Magyars, found in Dvorák and Smetana composers who could do for them what Chopin had done for the Poles and Liszt for the Hungarians. Music, the international language, could advertise national feelings. It may have

The Habsburg Dual Monarchy 1867

Portraits of composers from within the Habsburg monarchy who used traditional national themes in their music:

left: *Franz Liszt, 1811–86*

below left: *Bedrich Smetana, 1824–84*

below: *Antonin Dvorák 1841–1904*

seemed a shrewd move when the Habsburg government made a deal with the Hungarians, but it left the resentments of other nations within the Dual Monarchy to deepen.

The Russian Autocracy

The giant in the east remained undisturbed by liberal ideas, so it seemed. But though the educated classes of Russia were tiny in comparison with the great peasant masses, they produced in the nineteenth century a remarkable succession of musicians, poets, playwrights and novelists. These last particularly expressed deep concern at the futility and distress in which they saw many Russians, rich as well as poor, passing their lives. Some writers became victims of the censor, and spent years in exile, usually in Siberia.

The Tsar's state seemed vast and immovable. There seemed not the slightest hint that the Autocrat of All the Russias — such was one of his titles — or his entrenched host of officials would ever consider sharing some of their power with the people. This may partly explain why some Russian revolutionaries were so extreme. One picturesque figure, Count Michael Bakunin, preached *anarchism*. The idea was that if there were no governments, people would live in complete freedom and, therefore, happiness. They would form whatever groups they wanted for as long as they wanted, and they would not be corrupted and warped by the commands of their masters. There had been somewhat similar radical ideas published in France and Britain at various times since the late eighteenth century. The big difference was that now there were people who were ready to destroy everything connected with the society they lived in so that a fresh start could be made. Such people, because they wanted to preserve nothing (*nihil* in Latin), were called *nihilists*. Some of them were peaceful, wishing only to persuade by argument, but others thought it right to use the bullet and the bomb.

Yet changes might take place if the Autocrat himself thought them good. Had not Peter the Great changed Russia? Alexander II, who came to the throne in 1855, earned the nickname of the 'the Tsar Liberator'. In 1861 he signed an edict abolishing serfdom in Russia. Not only were the peasants freed, but each village community, or *mir*, kept the land it had worked. The mir was responsible for distributing the land among its members and for paying compensation to the former

masters. Three years later local councils, or *zemstvos*, were set up all over Russia. Their duty was to raise funds for local schools, hospitals and roads, and membership of the zemstvos was shared between the three classes of nobles, townsmen and peasants. In 1870 Alexander introduced elected town councils.

These reforms were not entirely successful. For example, some peasants found that as free men they were poorer and less protected than they had been as serfs with lords to look after them. But the Tsar had made an honest effort, and was willing to go further. On 13 March 1881 he agreed to a scheme for representatives of the zemstvos to help his government in framing laws, and obviously this might have led to some sort of Russian parliament. The same day the Tsar was murdered by revolutionaries. That stopped the reforms. The next Tsar and his advisers decided that unyielding strength was necessary to rule Russia. The bombers were probably pleased; they did not want reform, but hoped that things would come to such a pitch that there would be a violent revolution.

Alexander II had intended to give more freedom to his Polish subjects, too. In 1862 he restored to Poland the constitution lost as a result of the 1830 revolt. This pleased some

The murder of Alexander II caused a sensation throughout Europe. The 'Illustrated London News' devoted almost the whole of one issue to the event, and among the pictures was this reconstruction.

Poles, but many more felt encouraged to demand complete freedom from Russia. In January 1863 they rose. The governments of most other European states were inclined to sympathise with the Poles, partly because they would be glad to see Russia weakened. The nearest neighbour, though, was Prussia, where Bismarck saw his chance to show Russia what Prussian friendship was worth. With Prussian troops watching their long border with Poland, little support would reach the rebels from that direction. Russia felt safe in ignoring protests from Britain, France and Austria, and proceeded to stamp out the rising. It took the Russian army until May 1864 to finish their task, but then Poland was held more tightly by the Russian government even than after 1830.

Poles and Russians traditionally detested each other, though they were both Slav nations. In other directions the Russian government could manage to combine Tsarist imperial expansion, Russian nationalism, Pan-Slavism, and even Christian fervour in its policies. Across Central Asia the Tsar's armies were continually pushing, subduing ancient cities and nomad tribes and turning their peoples, who were mainly Muslim, into subjects of the Russian Empire. In the Balkans, Russia stood as the big cousin ready to defend Slav Christians if they were oppressed by the Sultan. When the other European governments were preoccupied with the Franco–German War in 1870, Russia took the opportunity to declare that she was no longer going to observe that part of the Paris Treaty (page 76) which forbade warlike preparations on the Black Sea. National feeling was strong among Russian and other Slavs, and this meant that Europe would hear more of the Eastern Question.

right: *Victoria in 1875, painted by Lady Abercrombie after H. von Angeli. The Queen wears a widow's veil, and a miniature of Albert is on her sleeve.*

below: *One of the results of the Industrial Revolution was a cheap, quick postal service. The first postage stamp was the 1840 British penny black; though the design of the stamp changed, a penny was the standard letter rate for the rest of Victoria's reign. Other countries soon copied the idea, and here are some stamps of the other main European powers round about 1870. The dates show when these designs were first issued.*

Austria 1867   France 1871   Germany 1872

Italy 1863   Russia 1864   Britain 1840

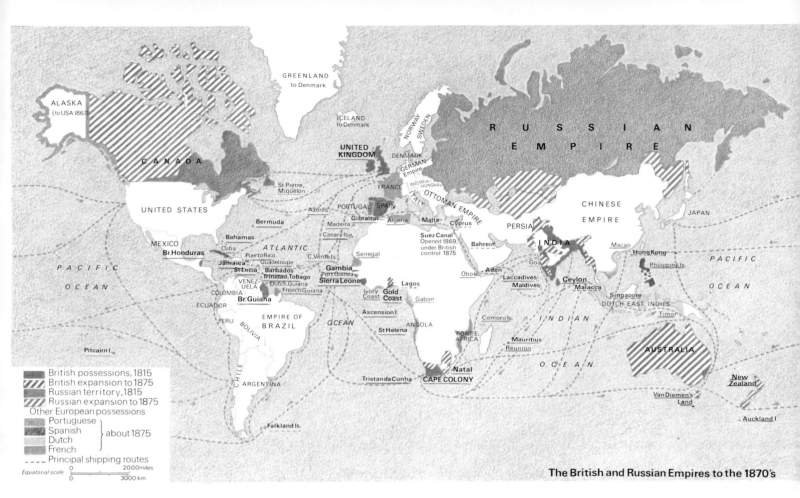

British possessions, 1815
British expansion to 1875
Russian territory, 1815
Russian expansion to 1875
Other European possessions
Portuguese
Spanish   } about 1875
Dutch
French
Principal shipping routes
Equatorial scale 0   2000 miles
                  0 3000 km

The British and Russian Empires to the 1870's

Victorian Britain

At the opposite end of Europe lay the British Isles, and Britain seemed Russia's opposite in many things besides geography. Britain's wealth was in industry and trade, and her armed strength was on the sea. The monarchy was constitutional, there was a steady flow of peaceful reforms and no attempts at violent revolution, and there were two great political parties which disagreed on many things but agreed in upholding the parliamentary system.

In the 1870s Victoria had been on the throne for more than a generation. Looking back, we can see that it was the middle of her reign, and may think of this as the most typically Vic-

torian time of all, when all the qualities we associate with the word were at their strongest. Whether or not that is a true judgment, it was not a good time for the queen herself. After the death of Prince Albert in 1861, Victoria dedicated herself to being a widow. She rarely appeared in public and she always dressed in black, though she still expected to be treated as a queen. There were some who said that the 'widow of Windsor' was not doing her duty, and even that Britain would be better as a republic. But these were also the years when British public life was dominated by the two mighty rivals, Disraeli and Gladstone, who between them held Britain steady.

Both of them had begun as Conservative M.P.s under Peel. Gladstone, whose family were solid Liverpool merchants of

Scottish descent, quickly became one of Peel's promising aides. In the crisis of 1846 he was one of the few who stood by Peel and broke with the other Conservatives. These 'Peelites' eventually joined with the Whigs and the few radical M.P.s to form the Liberal Party, with Gladstone as leader. Disraeli, on the other hand, began badly. He was (like Marx) Jewish by descent but not religion, conspicuously clever, conceited, flashy, and he wrote extravagant novels; none of these things endeared him to most Conservative M.P.s. But in the 1846 crisis he attacked 'traitor' Peel with such venom and polish that they began to see some good in him. Gradually they forgave him for not really being one of themselves, recognised his great ability, and at last made him leader of the Conservative Party.

The two men were a contrast. Disraeli was dry, sharp, cool, with a touch of irony even when pouring out flattery (as he did frequently, especially to the queen). Gladstone was large, earnest, emotional, manifestly religious and moral. He was given to making enormous eloquent thundering speeches that were sometimes so involved that their hearers were not sure of the meaning. The two men cordially disliked each other.

Between 1868 and 1885, Gladstone and Disraeli alternated as prime minister. In spite of—or because of—their rivalry, the two leaders were responsible for groups of acts which steadily increased the voting power of the ordinary people in electing M.P.s; gave them better prospects of improving their wages and working conditions; and tried to provide for the health, housing and education of even the poorest.

Two acts greatly extended the right to vote in parliamentary elections. In 1867 Disraeli, realising that the Conservatives could not resist the widespread demands for further reforms, and hoping that the new voters would be grateful to him, introduced a bill which increased the number of voters in England and Wales from one million to two. The qualification in the boroughs was broadened to include all taxpayers, and also lodgers paying £10 a year rent or more. In the counties, owners of land worth £5 and tenants paying £12 were included. The following year old seats were redistributed and new ones were created so that both the counties and the growing industrial areas got more M.P.s at the expense of the smaller boroughs. Disraeli's Reform Act gave the vote to a very large number of working men, and especially favoured those who worked in big towns. Gladstone's Reform Act came in 1884.

It extended the borough voting qualifications to cover the whole country, treating all men alike and ending the old distinction between shires and boroughs in Parliament. This doubled the electorate again. In 1885 Gladstone divided the country into constituencies with roughly equal numbers of voters in them. Since 1872 voting had been by secret ballot, which made bribery hardly worth while. Britain had proudly claimed to be the home of constitutional government, to have the 'mother of Parliaments', but recently it had seemed a hollow boast; many European countries allowed more of their people to vote. Now at least half the adult males in Britain had the vote, and if prosperity increased this proportion would probably increase too.

Having the vote meant that in the long run the ordinary people as a whole would have power over Parliament. M.P.s would try to please the greatest number of voters. But still only rich men could afford to be M.P.s. It was probably of much more practical use to working men when the laws about trade unions were altered, so that they could at last use the strength their numbers gave them in bargaining for better wages. Since the 1830s and 1840s unions had been careful and cautious, and most of them had been more like friendly societies of skilled workers, holding funds mainly to help members in time of illness and other misfortune. Because there was some doubt about their legal right to hold money, Gladstone in 1871 made it quite certain that they had such a right. In 1875 Disraeli went much further. He guaranteed that unions were entitled to strike, and that strikers could stand outside their workplaces and try to persuade other workers not to go in. This was called picketing, and was legal as long as it was done peacefully. Since 1868 representatives of different unions had been meeting every year in a congress, and after these acts there seemed nothing in the law to prevent trade unions from growing large, rich and powerful.

Both Liberals and Conservatives tried to improve conditions in different ways. Gladstone seemed particularly keen on providing people with the opportunities to help themselves, and with seeing that there was fair play. In 1870 the Education Act introduced by W. E. Forster set up local school boards all over the country to make sure that there were enough elementary schools available for every child to attend one. (Ten years later elementary education was made compulsory by the Liberals, and in 1891 it was made free of charge by the Con-

William Ewart Gladstone, 1809–98, and (right) Benjamin Disraeli, 1804–81, created Earl of Beaconsfield 1876. Both portraits were painted in the 1870s by the eminent Victorian artist Sir John Everett Millais, 1828–96.

servatives.) In 1870 also Gladstone ordered that candidates for most of the civil service should have to compete for places by examination, not simply be given jobs by the favour of some important person. Next year it was the army's turn. The act introduced by E. Cardwell brought about the end of the purchase system. This was the system that obliged an officer to pay a fee, every time he was promoted, to the man he replaced, which had meant that poorer officers sometimes could not afford higher and more expensive commands. The act also tried to link the army more with ordinary life. A soldier was now allowed to enlist for as short a period as six years, so that he did not need to cut himself off for most of his life from the civilians. Also the old infantry regiments were linked to particular counties, in the hope that this too would bring the army closer to the rest of the nation.

Disraeli's reforms were sometimes very down-to-earth. Public health had become a problem. As people crowded, diseases spread easily. Just how germs worked was not understood until Louis Pasteur (1822–95) in France and Robert Koch (1843–1910) in Germany published their researches, but it had long been realised that there was some connection between dirt and disease. After the cholera epidemic of 1831–2 Parliament had begun to take action. During the 1840s especially there were laws for removing 'nuisances', providing public baths and wash-houses, and setting up local boards to supervise sanitation. Fortunately, if the Industrial Revolution had increased dirt and overcrowding, it had also increased the power to provide reservoirs, pumps, pipes, cisterns, gratings, sewers. In 1875 Disraeli's Public Health Act brought together in one reasonably neat and complete system the pile of earlier acts. In the same year the Artisans' Dwelling Act gave local authorities the power to build houses for workmen. It was the first attempt by the government to find an answer to slums, though there had been attempts by other well-meaning people to encourage the design of good cheap houses.

On the whole, British reforms were practical and cheap. Usually the government did not have to find the money to pay for them; that was the duty of whichever community got the benefit of, say, a new school or drainage system. On the same principle, individuals had to contribute towards the cost of whatever they got, from elementary education to their tap-water. This was not simply because any government, Conservative or Liberal, wanted to keep taxes down. It was also because they saw a big difference between removing handicaps or giving opportunities for people to improve themselves, which was something the Victorians approved; and, on the other hand, doling out aid to idlers, which they despised. Many of the poor Victorians, as well as the comfortably off, saw 'charity' as a dreadful humiliation, and would sooner starve than accept it. Any responsible person, they thought, should rely on himself. There could be no improvement without effort.

This was more than ever the age of Progress. In 1859 a book entitled *The Origin of Species* was published. In it a scientist named Charles Darwin explained his theory of evolution. He explained it further in 1871, in *The Descent of Man*. His idea that men and apes were descended from the same ancestors seemed to many Christians to be an attack on both religion and the dignity of human beings, and there were furious controversies. At the same time, Darwin's theory of *natural selection*, or the survival of the fittest, could be taken as meaning that improvement was bound to go on for ever. Nothing, then, could stop Progress.

Certainly, anyone in the 1870s who looked back over the

Trade union membership certificate designed in 1866 for skilled men who obviously believed in the respectability, dignity and importance of their craft. Christ, 'Prince of Carpenters', presides over a mixture of realistic illustrations and the symbolic 'classic' figures of Industry and Art, Justice and Truth.

changes of the past century could hardly avoid believing in Progress. In so many ways human beings possessed powers which would have seemed miraculous to earlier generations. On land they could cover great distances at unheard-of speed by railway, and flash messages in an instant by telegraph line. At sea their iron steamships could ignore winds and currents, while telegraph cables crossed the ocean bed. Machines were weaving, hammering, printing, pulling with strength and speed that made human powers seem puny – but they were all serving mankind.

Admittedly, there were many millions of people who had as yet received no good from all these wonderful things. In southern and eastern parts of Europe itself, to say nothing of the other four continents, almost all the people were still labouring and living as they had for centuries. In the industrial countries themselves there were many who had suffered hardship. But surely the bad effects would cease before long, and the good effects spread wider!

Britain especially had been transformed, but so had a good part of Europe and other lands, notably the United States of America. Yet was it all this technical and economic development, or the political ideas which had been given explosive force by the French Revolution, which had done most to create the new Europe of the 1870s? The risings and revolts had failed, but out of their turmoil there had emerged great changes. Two big new powers, both nation-states, stretched over the centre of Europe; in most states national feeling seemed stronger than ever, often expressed and aroused by writers and musicians; and most governments, having agreed to rule according to a constitution and under the advice of an elected assembly or parliament, seemed to be recognising that the mass of the ordinary people of their nation was their ultimate source of power. They claimed power *from* the people, they claimed to be exerting their power *for* the people. Whether the ordinary people could ever possibly be able *themselves* to wield power was a question for the future.

Index

The Cambridge History Library

The Cambridge Introduction to History
Written by Trevor Cairns

PEOPLE BECOME CIVILIZED   EUROPE AND THE WORLD

THE ROMANS AND THEIR EMPIRE   THE BIRTH OF MODERN EUROPE

BARBARIANS, CHRISTIANS, AND MUSLIMS   THE OLD REGIME AND THE REVOLUTION

THE MIDDLE AGES   POWER FOR THE PEOPLE

The Cambridge Topic Books
General Editor Trevor Cairns

THE AMERICAN WAR OF INDEPENDENCE
by R. E. Evans

LIFE IN THE OLD STONE AGE
by Charles Higham

BENIN: AN AFRICAN KINGDOM AND CULTURE
by Kit Elliott

MARTIN LUTHER
by Judith O'Neill

THE BUDDHA
by F. W. Rawding

MEIJI JAPAN
by Harold Bolitho

BUILDING THE MEDIEVAL CATHEDRALS
by Percy Watson

THE MURDER OF ARCHBISHOP THOMAS
by Tom Corfe

THE EARLIEST FARMERS AND THE FIRST CITIES
by Charles Higham

MUSLIM SPAIN
by Duncan Townson

EARLY CHINA AND THE WALL
by P. H. Nancarrow

POMPEII
by Ian Andrews

THE FIRST SHIPS AROUND THE WORLD
by W. D. Brownlee

THE PYRAMIDS
by John Weeks

HERNAN CORTES: CONQUISTADOR IN MEXICO
by John Wilkes

THE ROMAN ARMY
by John Wilkes

LIFE IN A FIFTEENTH-CENTURY MONASTERY
by Anne Boyd

ST. PATRICK AND IRISH CHRISTIANITY
by Tom Corfe

LIFE IN THE IRON AGE
by Peter J. Reynolds

THE VIKING SHIPS
by Ian Atkinson

The Cambridge History Library will be expanded in the future to include additional volumes. Lerner Publications Company is pleased to participate in making this excellent series of books available to a wide audience of readers.